"This is a much-needed book that offers an important corrective to many common misunderstandings and puts a human face on those who serve in the registered church in China. Official statistics indicate there are more than thirty million members of registered churches, but little is known about their structure and how they function. Ten Harmsel, who served in and alongside registered churches in China for ten years, provides a glimpse of their inner workings. Based on conversations with pastors and leaders around the country, he allows us to hear directly about the unique challenges and opportunities they face."

—JOANN PITTMAN
Senior vice president at ChinaSource

"In engaging, easy-to-understand terms, Ten Harmsel draws together the latest scholarship on church-state relations in China with his own fresh perspectives to show readers what's happening at the grassroots of Chinese Christianity today. . . . After reading this book, readers will come away with surprising new insights: that church leaders are satisfied in the work they do and that seeing Chinese brothers and sisters as only suffering in 'persecuted churches' tells only a partial story. It gives any reader a bird's-eye view of important changes, a close-up understanding of new tensions in the Xi Jinping era, and a helpful understanding of how to walk beside and pray for brothers and sisters in the churches that are, as he writes, a 'gift and blessing to all in China.'"

—CARSTEN VALA
Chair of the Department of Political Science at Loyola University

"China's registered churches are the most accessible and visible churches in the country, so it is frustrating we know so little about them. Wayne Ten Harmsel has finally provided an intimate look into these congregations. He worked with them for years, and now allows his friends and colleagues to speak for themselves. This book paints the most lifelike portrait I have read to date."

—DARYL IRELAND
Associate director of the Center for Global Christianity and Mission,
Boston University

"Wayne Ten Harmsel's firsthand account and reflections on the Three-Self Churches is very enlightening. He dispels some misunderstandings about these congregations and their leaders and shows them to be largely pragmatic and evangelical in their beliefs and practice. Three-Self pastors, the author shows, focus on making the most of their opportunities to minister by finding ways to work around the restrictions imposed on them. In a climate of increasing government pressure, the registered churches make do by avoiding confrontations and focusing on personal salvation and discipleship. Ten Harmsel has traveled extensively in China and visited with more than a hundred Three-Self congregations. He offers rare glimpses into the thought and practice of these, the most public and accessible but often overlooked Chinese Christians."

—JOEL A. CARPENTER
Nagel Institute, Calvin University

"Readers of Wayne Ten Harmsel's *The Registered Churches in China* will find it very timely. The relationship between the Chinese government and religions, especially Christianity, is undergoing changes almost as momentous as the changes of 1980, following the end of the Cultural Revolution. . . . The author has a wealth of on-the-ground experience with the Christian churches about which he writes. . . . While more has been written on the unregistered 'house' churches, the story of the registered (legal) churches is equally important to the overall history of Protestantism in recent Chinese history. Ten Harmsel's main aim in the book is to make up for this imbalance. . . . His ability to speak as an insider, and to have access to the other insiders whom he was able to interview for the book, makes the book uniquely valuable. . . . Filled with vignettes of Ten Harmsel's interactions with religious people, government officials, and others he encounters in his many travels throughout China, the book has entertainment as well as historical value. Those fortunate enough to encounter it will find it a joy to read."

—CHRISTIAN JOCHIM
Professor emeritus at San Jose State University

THE REGISTERED CHURCH IN CHINA

Studies in Chinese Christianity

G. Wright Doyle and Carol Lee Hamrin,
Series Editors

A Project of the Global China Center

www.globalchinacenter.org

Previously published volumes in the series

Carol Lee Hamrin & Stacey Bieler, eds., *Salt and Light: Lives of Faith That Shaped Modern China*, volume 1

Carol Lee Hamrin & Stacey Bieler, eds., *Salt and Light: More Lives of Faith That Shaped Modern China*, volume 2

Richard R. Cook & David W. Pao, eds., *After Imperialism: Christian Identity in China and the Global Evangelical Movement*

Carol Lee Hamrin & Stacey Bieler, *Salt and Light: More Lives of Faith That Shaped Modern China*, volume 3

Lit-sen Chang, *Wise Man from the East: Lit-sen Chang (Zhang Lisheng)*

George Hunter McNeur, *Liang A-Fa: China's First Preacher, 1789–1855*

Eunice V. Johnson, *Timothy Richard's Vision: Education and Reform in China, 1880–1910*

G. Wright Doyle, *Builders of the Chinese Church: Pioneer Protestant Missionaries and Chinese Church Leaders*

Jack R. Lundbom, *On the Road to Siangyang: Covenant Mission in Mainland China 1890–1949*

Brent Fulton, *China's Urban Christians: A Light That Cannot Be Hidden*

Andrew T. Kaiser, *The Rushing on of the Purposes of God: Christian Missions in Shanxi since 1876*

Li Ma & Jin Li, *Surviving the State, Remaking the Church: A Sociological Portrait of Christians in Mainland China*

Linda Banks and Robert Banks, *Through the Valley of the Shadow: Australian Women in War-Torn China*

Arthur Lin, *The History of Christian Missions in Guangxi, China*

Linda Banks and Robert Banks, *They Shall See His Face: The Story of Amy Oxley Wilkinson and Her Visionary Work among the Blind in China*

THE REGISTERED CHURCH IN CHINA

Flourishing in a Challenging Environment

WAYNE TEN HARMSEL

PICKWICK *Publications* · Eugene, Oregon

THE REGISTERED CHURCH IN CHINA
Flourishing in a Challenging Environment

Pickwick Publications
An Imprint of Wipf and Stock Publishers
199 W. 8th Ave., Suite 3
Eugene, OR 97401

www.wipfandstock.com

PAPERBACK ISBN: 978-1-7252-8622-1
HARDCOVER ISBN: 978-1-7252-8623-8
EBOOK ISBN: 978-1-7252-8624-5

Cataloguing-in-Publication data:

Names: Ten Harmsel, Wayne, author.

Title: The registered church in China : flourishing in a challenging environment / Wayne Ten Harmsel.

Description: Eugene, OR: Pickwick Publications, 2021 | Studies in Chinese Christianity. | Includes bibliographical references.

Identifiers: ISBN 978-1-7252-8622-1 (paperback). | ISBN 978-1-7252-8623-8 (hardcover). | ISBN 978-1-7252-8624-5 (ebook).

Subjects: LCSH: Christianity—China. | Communism and Christianity—China.

Classification: BR1285 T46 2021 (paperback). | BR1285 (ebook).

03/01/21

For Pastor Du Fengying,
who made it all possible.

Contents

Acknowledgments

DURING THE YEARS I served as a missionary in China, people frequently suggested that I write a book about the experience. For a long time, I ignored them. But after my retirement, as more and more people joined in the encouragement, I could not help but consider. I knew I did not have any desire to write another standard missionary biography. At the same time, I knew that the registered churches, with whom I worked, were not receiving a fair shake from Christians both inside and outside of China. So, I decided to write a book that I hoped would shed light on these brothers and sisters and their churches.

During my years in China, I received constant help navigating the language and understanding the society and churches from "Water," my first language teacher in Beijing, as well as from my colleague Lorraine Li, and friends Bao Shengjie and Ma Hongbing. The book would lack any substance were it not for the many pastors and evangelists I interviewed. The majority of these were unknown to me and yet graciously gave me their attention and their wisdom when I asked about their lives and their churches. I am especially thankful to several pastors in Beijing whom I am honored to count as friends.

This book would have been much impoverished without help from Mary Ma, Emily Brink, Joann Pittman, Christian Jochim, and Daryl Ireland, all of whom read the manuscript and made valuable suggestions. Special thanks are due to two people who went out of their way to help. Wright Doyle shepherded me through much of the pre-publication jungle, encouraging me along the way. This book would be much less interesting and harder to read without benefiting from the editorial skills of Bette Vandinther, who also encouraged me when I was down or frustrated by reminding me of the value of the book. I also need to acknowledge that any remaining mistakes or misunderstandings are mine alone.

Finally, I thank my wife, Lin Baoyu. This is more than just a cliché tacked on to the end of the acknowledgements. Without her patience through years of urging me to write this book, without her constantly reminding me to get to work, without her reassurances that what I was writing was good and necessary to write, without her prayers, this book would never have come to fruition. I thank God for you!

Wayne Ten Harmsel

Grand Rapids

2020

Introduction

As 2017 FADED INTO 2018, a sense of foreboding hung over Christians in China. The government had issued new regulations on church activities. Among other things, the regulations came down hard on foreign involvement, home meetings, and religious activities off of church property. Such activities had always been illegal, but now the government seemed ready to enforce religious regulations as they never had before. While it is too early to tell with any certainty, the consensus among local and Western observers is that the regulations will make life and ministry more difficult, especially for unregistered churches.

When the Communist Party took over China in 1949, they required that all religious groups be registered. For Protestant churches, that meant participating in, or as some would say, being controlled by, the *Lianghui*, translated as Two Councils or Two Committees. These two councils, one called The Three-Self Patriotic Movement (self-governing, self-propagating, self-supporting) and the other called The Christian Council, were officially formed in 1954, and together became the governing bodies of the Protestant church in China.

Not surprisingly, many churches refused to register with the *Lianghui*. These unregistered churches became known as house churches, and because they were illegal, they had no voice in the *Lianghui* and no protection from overt oppression by the Chinese government. The regulations that went into effect in February of 2018 have notably been targeted at these unregistered churches, enough so that house church pastors voice fear of a return to the oppression and persecution that they endured during the Cultural Revolution years (1966–76). Both registered and unregistered pastors have reported the bulldozing of hundreds of meeting places and the removal of thousands of crosses. Some pastors and outspoken leaders have been arrested, and prominent unregistered churches like Zion Church in Beijing and Early Rain Church in Chengdu have been shuttered. In rural areas and small towns, even registered churches are beginning to feel the pressure.

Protestant missionaries have played a significant role in the growth of unregistered churches in China, and their impact has been recorded in numerous articles and books. Many nondenominational organizations, such as China Partnership, Open Doors, and Voice of the Martyrs, are devoted to collecting and disseminating information about the unregistered churches in China.[1] In contrast, less has been reported about the growth and wellbeing of the churches that chose to register with the *Lainghui*. First, being a missionary has always been illegal in China, so missionaries who did come, primarily from the West and from Korea, saw the underground church communities as their mission partners. They would arrive in China as employees in various commercial companies or agencies, and then covertly spread the gospel, setting up covert house groups of Christians along the way. Information, therefore, about mission work in China comes naturally from these missionaries, while, in contrast, information about registered churches remains local and rarely gets out of China.

Second, the information that does get reported about registered churches is primarily from members, missionaries, and pastors of unregistered churches who often display a negative, even hostile, attitude toward the members and pastors of registered churches. Naturally, the news they send home praises and supports the unregistered churches while criticizing the duplicity of the registered churches whom they accuse of selling out to the government and, coincidentally, promoting liberal theology. The story of the registered churches in China, then, is somewhat of a black hole to Western Christians. Nothing is known about them except for the popular complaints that serve only to foster continued mistrust and divisiveness amongst Christians both inside and outside of China.

And finally, the Chinese are world experts at bureaucracy. They have roughly three thousand years (they will tell you it is more like six thousand years) of experience at layers and layers of bureaucracy. The registered churches are unavoidably part of that bureaucracy. When talking with officials, code words are rife, layers of meaning are multiple, and a clear explanation is often hard to come by.

My purpose is to report on the status and wellbeing of the registered churches in China. In 2008, I was told that there were more than seventy thousand registered churches in China and their numbers were increasing every year. They are a force to be reckoned with in the religious landscape

---

1. Among these, only *ChinaSource* includes news about the registered church as well.

of China. I hope to correct some of the misinformation, clear away some of the myths, offer accurate information about the challenges, failings, and successes of the registered churches in China, and contribute to a new conversation.

The rift between the registered and unregistered churches was apparent already in the early twentieth century during what has often been called the high point of Protestant missions in China. In his book, *A New History of Christianity in China*, Daniel Bays describes an era in which Western missions became well established and well funded, focusing on building and running schools, hospitals, seminaries, and churches. He calls this movement the "Sino-Foreign Protestant Establishment." The foreign part of this "establishment" was mostly from the more liberal or progressive mainline churches and other organizations such as the YMCA. This was not any sort of organized movement, but rather a loosely allied group that represented a directional vision for Chinese Christianity.[2] The Three-Self ideology of self-governing, self-propagating, and self-supporting had a small beginning in the late nineteenth century with the support of a few of these missionaries and allied Chinese believers. While the intention of this movement was to establish complete Chinese leadership for the local church, that goal would never be fully attained.

During the same period, missionaries with a different vision arrived in China. The fundamentalist, revivalist movement was made up of foreign missionaries from conservative churches and agencies, especially the China Inland Mission. In the 1920s these two groups' attitudes towards each other clashed and hardened,[3] and, in spite of various efforts at promoting unity, these groups continued to push apart. When the Communists marched triumphantly into Beijing in October of 1949, the church was already divided into these two camps. Those in the Sino-Foreign Protestant Establishment chose to work with the new government, and they re-cast the Three-Self Patriotic Movement into a body overseen by both the government and the church. They quickly found themselves, however, firmly under the control of the government and they watched helplessly as virtually all missionaries were expelled and their hospitals and schools were taken over by the government. Meanwhile, the fundamentalist, conservative, revivalist Christians, fueled by their brethren's sell-out to the atheistic government, chose to vehemently oppose the Communists and were forced to go underground. Although there were already differences between the two movements in missiology, theology, and social action, this divide fostered subsequent

2. Bays, *A New History of Christianity in China*, 99–103.

3. Bays, *A New History of Christianity in China*, 104–06.

bitterness, mistrust, and even betrayal. In the 1950s and early 1960s, some Three-Self pastors were said to have helped the government locate pastors and other Christians who were in hiding.[4] The polarization escalated during the decade-long Cultural Revolution when all churches were shuttered and all Christians had to go underground. Now as a completely covert and underground movement, the social, political, and theological identity of Chinese Christians as a house church community was forged.

In the late 1970s, as China sought to recover from the oppressive policies of the Cultural Revolution, the registered churches were allowed to reopen. By this time, however, its members were few, poor, and overwhelmingly rural. Both economically and socially, thirty years of government oppression had beaten people down so that no one was optimistic about any kind of church growth.

By the mid 1980s, more change was in the air as Deng Xiaoping, the new Premier of China, initiated a program of "reform and opening." He reestablished foreign trade, which led to a new middle class with secure jobs, rising income, and extra money to spend. For the first time in centuries, people could work to buy their own homes, cars, TVs, and more. Along with foreign trade came foreign ideas, and one of those ideas was Christianity, not actually new, but re-presented, re-imagined. People could see that Christians in other countries were not necessarily old and poor and backwards, and surprisingly to many, Christianity gave satisfying answers to the deep questions people were asking.

Registered church leaders and pastors were also changing; they were younger, theologically more conservative, more urban, better trained, and were attracting younger, more urban parishioners. For this new leadership, the disagreements and bitterness of the past were not as important as was their vision for a church that could be meaningful for a new generation of Chinese youth.

I lived in China from 2006 to 2017 and took extended trips there in 2018 and 2019. I was sent by the Christian Reformed Church in North America, commissioned to work with the registered churches and only in ways that were approved by those churches. Under these guidelines, my colleagues and I ran Summer Vacation Bible Schools for all ages, led Timothy Leadership Training Conferences, and taught at seminars for lay leaders in several churches. We also recruited and translated for foreign scholars lecturing at the seminary. We led many small group Bible studies, taught various courses at seminaries, and led Sunday School teacher training classes all

---

4. Bays discusses this in more detail in *A New History of Christianity in China*, 158–68.

over China. We also accompanied Chinese pastors and seminary professors to conferences in the US. I know of only a handful of others doing this sort of work in China. It seemed a daunting challenge at first, but over my twelve years there, as the layers of bureaucracy and confusion became more manageable to me, and as my work and contributions there became productive and fruitful, I learned to understand, love, and appreciate the Christian friends who work every day in the Lord's name in the registered churches in China.

I regard this small book, in one sense, as the reflections of a missionary looking back on a dozen or so years working in China, and in another sense, as a report on the condition of the Christian church in China as it reacts and adapts to an aggressive Communist government bent on hurling China into the modern world. I do not come to this study in the totally objective fashion of the academic; a good number of the interviewees for this book are close personal friends and brothers and sisters in Christ. I do hope, however, that those with a more academic interest will find it useful, especially because it focuses on an area in which little scholarly work has been done.

A few caveats regarding this study: For nearly all of my time in China, I was in Beijing, although I did take part in some ministry in the provinces of Hunan, Shandong, Liaoning, and Fujian. Consequently, most of what I write is based on my experience in Beijing. I am cognizant of the truism that China is a vast and complex country, and what is true in one place may not be so in another, and this book is not meant to be an exhaustive or generalizable study even of the registered church in Beijing, much less the whole country. That is quite likely an impossible task. Additionally, I have limited knowledge of the unregistered churches, and I report on them only as a contrast and comparison with what I know to be true of the registered churches.

My sources are interviews with pastors, church leaders, and lay people whom I met and worked with during my twelve years in China, interviews with pastors I met while on a church visit trip across China from south to north in 2011, and church leaders whom I worked with while I conducted summer programs. I have also resourced relevant published material. The people I interviewed were mostly senior pastors, ranging from those who had been serving their churches for over twenty years to those who were newly out of seminary. Most of these pastors were in their 30s or 40s. Some had studied at the seminary in Beijing, others at Jinling Seminary in Nanjing, and a few at overseas seminaries. Some were pastors in local churches, while others held the highest positions in the local, provincial, and national church governing bodies. I also interviewed lay leaders who performed many of the duties of pastors, as well as committee members or members actively involved in their local churches.

I would like to note that almost without exception, the pastors and lay leaders were satisfied in the work they were doing. Given the challenges of being a pastor in China at this time, one might expect otherwise, but they felt called by God to their positions. They felt God's hand of blessing on them and were encouraged by their own spiritual growth and that of their congregations. Being a pastor, no matter the difficulties, was worthwhile and important to them.

Throughout this study, I rely on translations I have made (not direct quotes) from conversations I had with Chinese clergy and churchgoers in Beijing (and elsewhere if noted). The translations are not word-for-word, and unless my interviewees wish to be identified or are already well-known, I intentionally do not name individuals or present personal information that might identify them. Given that their words as I have them could jeopardize not only their positions but, more important, their safety, I do what I can to preserve individuals' anonymity. As a result, in the translation paraphrases that follow not even I always know specifically who has said what.

Each chapter of this book begins with a section taken from the journal I kept while travelling from Yunnan Province in the south to the town of Hegang on the Russian border in the north. During my five-week trip, I visited about thirty churches. I did not take this trip at the instruction of my sending agency, but they were supportive of the undertaking. I did not plan out a detailed itinerary, but my goal was to focus on small to medium-sized cities, to travel by bus or train, and to stay close to the middle of China. I made no appointments with pastors and usually did not even know which church I would be visiting until the day I arrived. Amazingly, I was able to talk with a pastor or church leader in all but three cities. The journal entries are not meant to illustrate or explain the content of the chapter, although there may sometimes be connections. Rather, these are intended to give readers a small taste of life in China and its churches, and of my adventures on the road.

While my work focuses mostly on Protestant churches, I do not discount the legacy of the Roman Catholic Church in China. Their presence goes back to about 1582, when Matteo Ricci, an Italian Jesuit priest, arrived in southern China. In 1601, he moved to Beijing and established a mission base there. The Roman Catholic Church in China has had its own tumultuous history ever since, but has remained a vibrant presence in the Chinese church world. Following the Communist takeover in 1949, the Roman Catholic Church, like the Protestant church, split into two camps, the registered and the unregistered churches. As with the Protestants, the

fundamental issue was government control, which became further complicated by the Roman Catholic insistence of primary papal authority. In
the registered Roman Catholic churches, the pope had no means by which
to claim authority. In general, church leadership in these churches was in
the hands of the local church and government officials. In the unregistered
churches, however, papal authority could be recognized as the agency that
approved and appointed local priests. As of 2018, the government and the
churches supposedly reached an agreement that gave both sides a role in
the appointment of priests, bishops, etc., but this has yet to be successfully
implemented.[5]

The plan of the book is as follows: Chapter 1 is an introduction to the
registered church. What are its core doctrines? What is its worship like?
What programs does it offer? What are the demographics of its congregations? How does it engage in outreach? Other questions are more organizational: How is the church structured and operated? How many and what
sort of pastors are there? Is there a church ruling body? Are there elders and
deacons? Where does authority lie? How are finances handled? Answers to
these questions will of course vary from church to church, but are generally homogeneous. This chapter also explores some of the workings of the
Lianghui, which provides governmental oversight at local, provincial, and
national levels.

Chapter 2 is a description and analysis of the changes, challenges, and
limitations faced by the church. The church in China exists in the face of
many challenges and pressures. These include attacks from cults of various
kinds, less than ideal preparation of pastors for their work, a critical shortage of pastors and biblical scholars, frequent attacks from unregistered
fellowships, rising expectations of the members, and an astoundingly low
level of biblical and theological knowledge on the part of a large number of
lay people. Ecclesiastical isolation is also a problem. Although occasionally
Western religious leaders come to visit, any real connection or cooperation
is strictly limited by the government and by the preconceptions of Western
Christians.

Chapter 3 explores complicated church-government relations. On a
formal level, these relations are carried on through the *Lianghui*, and one of
the ironies of church-state relations is that the churches are overseen by this
quasi-governmental body, many of whose members are not believers. How
does this affect the day-by-day functioning of the church? Are there ways in
which the government sets the ground rules for the ministry and limits the

---

5. For readers interested in the history of the Catholic Church in China, a good
place to start is Bays, *A New History of Christianity in China*. While Bays focuses on the
Protestant Church, he also includes sections about the Catholic Church.

scope of outreach? Does the government block the work of the pastors and members? Conversely, are the pastors able to influence the government? And the key question of this study: How do Christians go about being the church of Jesus Christ under these conditions? The answers to these questions may take some by surprise. The relationship between church and state is not simply that of ruler and ruled. It is much more complicated.

Chapter 4 reviews the new regulations regarding religion. These regulations were first published in mid-2017 and officially took effect on February 1, 2018. Much depends upon to what extent the government, national and local, will enforce the new regulations. Some registered church pastors have different ideas regarding these regulations.

Chapter 5 studies the "Sinicization" of Christianity. Ever since the Apostle Paul said he would become all things to all people in order to save some, Christianity has been involved in contextualization and indigenization. Ed Stetzer puts it this way in *Christianity Today:*

> We should hope to see and work to create indigenous expressions of gospel-centered, mission-shaped churches. And contextualization is part of the process that moves us toward indigenization. As I have said earlier, the work of contextualization creates tension. Without contextualization, we end up with an unintelligible gospel. Without ongoing contextualization, we end up living out cultural forms and believing that they are the gospel.[6]

Is the Sinicization of Christianity in China simply contextualization? Or is it a sinister attempt by the Chinese government to change the very nature and beliefs of Christians and make Christianity conform to and support Chinese socialism? The answer to that question depends on whom you talk to and what you read.

Chapter 6 turns to the equally complicated nature of the relationship between registered and unregistered (house) churches. Outside observers often characterize the relationship as hopeless and unyielding. Unregistered church leaders are often critical of the registered church, criticizing its theology as liberal, its relationship with the government as sinful, and concluding that one cannot be saved in the registered church. The registered church, meanwhile, either ignores the unregistered churches or criticizes them as being a breeding ground for cults and anarchist movements in the broader Christian community. Again, while these negative attitudes and resentments persist, there are pastors and churches from both sides who are reaching out and working for closer relations.

6. Stetzer, "Calling for Contextualization."

Chapter 7 again asks the question: How can a church be the church in a repressive and antagonistic setting? Further, what are the strengths and weaknesses of the registered church? Is the registered church in China succeeding at being the church in its unique and challenging environment? What measures does one use to arrive at answers to these questions?

And finally, the Conclusion asks about the future for the church in China. We so easily cast stones from the safe distance of our Western comfort, security, and freedom. The Chinese church exists in a different but real world where the Spirit of God is not about politics and where the Christian church is a gift and a blessing for all of China. How do we walk beside these brothers and sisters in Christ?

Wayne Ten Harmsel
Beijing
September 2019

Abbreviations

CC: Christian Council

RAB: Religious Affairs Bureau

RMB: Renminbi (Chinese currency)

SARA: State Administration of Religious Affairs

SDA: Seventh Day Adventist Church

TSPM: Three-Self Patriotic Movement

UFWD: United Front Work Department

VBS: Vacation Bible School

Abbreviations

CC   Christian Council

1

We Are Christ's Church!

Journal Entry, June 10, 2011, Kunming, Yunnan Province

Today in Kunming, intermittent rain and thunderstorms soaked my clothes and hampered my plans. I was able to make it to Trinity International Church, a large, traditional Western-style church building, hard to miss even among the tall, nondescript apartment and office buildings. I met with Pastor Deng, an evangelist who had graduated from Yanjing Seminary in Beijing, and was on her way to becoming an ordained pastor. She told me that Trinity International is the largest registered church in Yunnan Province. In addition to housing the church, the building is home to the Yunnan provincial Three-Self offices. This Saturday morning, a worship service was in progress. This church offers four services per week, including this one and three on Sundays. The sanctuary seats from one thousand five hundred to two thousand worshipers and all services are usually full. Pastor Deng told me that at each baptism service (three per year) two hundred to three hundred people are baptized. I asked her how the church made room for all these new people, and she mentioned a number of things: Because of work schedules, some people are not able to make it to a worship service regularly; some who are baptized at Trinity eventually go to other churches, either in Kunming or elsewhere; some attend other services (like the youth service) and may not attend a Sunday worship. The church recently added a Saturday service to accommodate more people. Trinity has only two ordained pastors, along with a number of evangelists and others who preach.

Much of the pastoral care is done by volunteers. In addition to an English Bible study, this church offers a weekly class and worship time for the disabled, as well as a similar class specifically for the blind.[1]

In the summer of 2011, I spent two months traveling from Kunming City in southern China to the town of Hegang on the Russian border in the north, visiting registered churches and interviewing pastors. Every pastor I met talked about the label that their church lived with and could not shake. Their churches were referred to as "Three-Self Churches," referencing those churches that had registered with the government and were part of an organization called the Three-Self Patriotic Movement. The Three-Self, they said, did not define their church; Jesus Christ defined their church. The Three-Self Patriotic Movement simply provided a bridge between State and church so that dialogue was possible.

Myths abound regarding the registered churches.[2] Perhaps the most common is the claim that registered church pastors need to have their sermons approved by the government. The pastors I questioned about this first had a good laugh and then vigorously denied the claim. More than one opined about how an atheist government official would not know how to pass judgment on a Christian sermon. One pastor summed up all of their answers: "In twenty years of being a pastor, I have never had the government tell me what to preach and teach." Another added that if a pastor does say something questionable, members of the congregation, not government officials, will call them out. It is possible and does happen, that government agents sit in on church services, but in my experience, I have never heard of a registered church pastor who has gotten into trouble over the contents of a sermon. I can add my own testimony here that I have preached at least one hundred times in China and never had my sermons scrutinized.

A related myth is that registered church pastors may not preach on the second coming of Christ, the book of Daniel, or the book of Revelation. This is also not true. In addition to the critique of congregants, each

1. As I noted in the introduction, throughout this study, I rely on translations I have made from conversations I had with Chinese clergy and churchgoers in Beijing (and elsewhere if noted). The translations are not word-for-word, and unless my interviewees wish to be identified or are already well-known, I intentionally do not name individuals or present personal information that might identify them. Given that their words as I have them could jeopardize not only their positions but, more important, their safety, I do what I can to preserve individuals' anonymity. As a result, in the translation paraphrases that follow not even I always know specifically who has said what.

2. The word "myth" is, at times, used pejoratively to imply that a belief is based on supernatural beings or events, but I am using the word only to refer to a false or uninformed notion about a situation.

congregation has a committee called the *shigongzu,* an informal group of volunteers consisting of several mature believers, which checks sermons. This might be similar to the responsibilities of elders in many Protestant churches.

A more serious claim charges that registered church pastors are liberal in their theology. However, China scholar Nathan Faries, in his book, *The "Inscrutably Chinese" Church,* describes them as "overwhelmingly evangelical,"[3] and my experience affirms this. Yet another myth claims that registered churches simply do not do meaningful ministry. I agree, however, with Chinese Christianity scholars Alan Hunter and Kim-Kwong Chan, who address this charge:

> As regards the Protestant church, much religious activity is conducted openly and freely. The sacraments of adult baptism and communion; preaching, prayer, and hymn-singing; Bible study and training courses; celebration of festivals; private devotion; and distribution of religious literature; all these take place in thousands of churches throughout China.[4]

Yet another charge is that registered church pastors are "in it for the money." Since registered church pastors do generally earn more than their counterparts in unregistered churches, this claim might have some truth to it, but no pastors go into ministry in China to get rich. Salaries for pastors in the larger cities average about 2,500 RMB (about $350) per month, roughly equivalent to the pay for an entry level office job, while salaries in small towns and rural areas may be about 1,000 RMB. Often, pastors are not paid at all.

WORSHIP

Congregational worship is the heart of any church, and registered churches in China are impressively typical and traditional in their worship format. When I first arrived in Beijing in 2006, the church my wife and I attended had the following worship order:

- Worship Song Practice
- Prelude
- Choir, Liturgist, and Preacher Processional

3. Faries, *"Inscrutably Chinese" Church,* 244.
4. Hunter, *Protestantism in Contemporary China,* 53.

- Call to Worship—usually from the Psalms
- Hymn—usually a translation of an old Western hymn
- Congregational Prayer by Liturgist
- Responsive Reading—usually a Psalm
- Hymn
- Congregational Recitation of the Lord's Prayer
- Reading of Scripture
- Choir Anthem
- Sermon—at least thirty minutes, prayer before and after
- Welcoming of First-time Visitors—short song to welcome them
- Communion or Baptism—on designated Sundays
- Announcements
- Hymn
- Benediction

When I returned to China in 2019, not much had changed. Most churches I have attended are remarkably similar. Some may add the Apostles Creed, some may have a time of open prayer, some may have longer (or shorter) sermons, some may use newer music, but that is all. The majority of churches use the same hymnal, the *New Songs of Praise*, which is comprised of mostly traditional Western hymns, but also includes many new and indigenous songs. All use the same Bible version, the *Heheben*, or Union Version.[5] The services remind me of worship in the 1950s in the church in which I grew up. Possibly the Chinese church was frozen in time when it was closed down in the 1960s and 1970s during the Cultural Revolution, or this could be a holdover from the days of the Western missionaries of the nineteenth and early twentieth centuries. Worship in the registered churches certainly cannot be accused of being innovative! Most of their practices are the same as those of many other Christian churches, although some practices are distinctly Chinese. On the positive side, the weight of these traditional worship services serves as a unifying force for churches all over the country.

Youth services, likewise, follow the predictable format of the "contemporary worship" models from the United States and South Korea. They

---

5. In the past couple of years, I have seen the occasional use of new songs from the supplement to the *Lianghui*-approved hymnal as well as the use of a new Bible translation.

open with about thirty minutes of singing, generally of newer music, accompanied by a band, and led by one or more worship leaders. The sermon follows, after which people are dismissed with a blessing. The youth services are open to any age, and many older folks do attend. Perhaps the time fits their schedule better, or perhaps, just like in many churches around the world, some older people attend the youth services because they prefer the freer, more expressive worship.

The sacraments are important in all churches. In Beijing's Gangwashi Church, baptism is administered three times per year, Easter Sunday, a midsummer Sunday, and a Sunday close to Christmas. Many other churches have baptism just twice per year. Generally, in Beijing and many other large cities, baptism is administered by sprinkling, although immersion is also offered. In rural areas immersion is more popular, especially in the summer. Children are not typically baptized, only adult new believers, although one pastor told me that if infant baptism is requested, it will be accommodated. The number of people baptized at each of these services is stunning. When I first arrived in 2006, there were about one hundred fifty baptized at each of these three services in the church we attended. Now, thirteen years later, it has decreased somewhat although seventy-five to one hundred is not unusual. Some churches baptize around two thousand per year! In most churches, new Christians must go through a process in order to be baptized, although this varies somewhat from church to church. The applicant must have been attending church for a minimum of a year, request to be baptize, attend a class on the basics of the faith, and have an interview with one of the pastors. Baptism, as with Communion and the Benediction, may only be administered by ordained pastors.

The Lord's Supper is celebrated, often the first Sunday of each month, with elements distributed to people in their seats. Most churches have no set liturgy for this other than Paul's words in 1 Corinthians 11. The elements are distributed by *yigong*, or lay leaders, who have been chosen and trained for that position. Those who have not yet been baptized are warned by the pastor against participating. One additional policy affected me personally: Foreigners, even if ordained, may not officiate at communion.[6]

In Beijing and other large cities, churches often have multiple Sunday worship services. The liturgy at these services is normally identical, except that the sermons are different since different pastors are preaching. Typically, churches hold two or three morning services and one evening service. I was told that this was the practical way to deal with all the newcomers.

---

6. This is why it was very meaningful for me when I was asked by a church in Fujian to help officiate at communion.

Since land is scarce and expensive, the building of more structures is impractical. And, conveniently, the government finds it easier to control one large church than many small churches. Even with multiple services, the twenty large churches in Beijing are not able to accommodate all the believers, so worship is provided in alternative venues, in *juhuidian*, or "meeting points." These are similar to house churches, but are registered and more or less officially connected to one of the "big" churches. They can range from a dozen or so people gathered in a house to a hundred or more in a rented space. A pastor at one large church said that about forty of these smaller groups are connected to his church. Some large churches may be affiliated with more than one hundred *juhuidian*. These groups generally have no pastor, but are served on a rotating basis by pastors or lay leaders from their parent church. I have talked with several lay leaders who preached in these house churches, and recently, I accompanied a pastor in a coastal city for a weeknight worship service. About fifteen people met in a rented apartment. The service opened with a time of singing and was followed by a traditional worship service. The church even had a choir that included more than half the people there! This particular *juhuidian*, the pastor told me, had been in existence for more than twenty years.

Preaching is problematic in many registered churches. Sermons are often moralistic, using scriptural stories and characters to say, in effect, "We need to be like David," or "We need to have faith like Peter." I have heard pastors get so bogged down in the minutest details about Bible characters and customs and geography that they completely lost the focus of the sermon. I have heard any number of sermons that never mentioned Jesus. It's not that these sermons are heretical; they just miss the point. In addition, spiritual content is often lacking. The sermons are typically aimed at the head, not the heart. That having been said, it's also true that some of the best sermons I have heard were in Beijing.

BELIEFS

The registered church has often been accused of promoting liberal theology. While that may be true for a few leaders, particularly those at the top of the *Lianghui* bureaucracy, the great majority of pastors are not at all liberal. It would be more accurate to describe most of the churches as theologically similar to conservative evangelical churches in the United States, although just like churches in the US, a range of beliefs exists. One pastor told me that in the US, churches have denominational signs on the outside of the building, but in China the signs are inside of each pastor and believer.

Some pastors follow the teachings of a Chinese Christian Pentecostal teacher, Jing Dianying. In the early 1900s, he established a church called The Jesus Family that became popular and well established in rural communities. His followers practiced simple living, spiritual inspirations, and longing for the Second Coming of Christ. In 1952, however, the church was dismantled by the Communist Party, Jing was imprisoned, and his followers went underground.[7] Other pastors I met expressed an interest in Reformed theology.

On the whole, registered church pastors hold to such basic beliefs as God's creation of the universe, man's fall into sin, and the incarnation and virgin birth of Jesus Christ. They profess his atonement for our sins, suffering and death on the cross, resurrection and ascension, rule at the right hand of God the Father, and coming again in judgment and glory, as well as the physical reality of Heaven and Hell, and the outpouring of the Holy Spirit on believers. In twelve years of listening to sermons in registered churches, I have not heard one that I would describe as liberal.

The charge of liberalism stems, at least partially, from the early days of the People's Republic. At that time, the more liberal pastors and leaders were willing to work with the government, and they then became the nucleus and the voice of the Three-Self Patriotic Movement.[8] In the eyes of many Christians, the TSPM remains forever linked to liberalism and to collusion with the enemy. While the old reputation lingers on, the new reality is that a new generation of pastors, now in their thirties and forties, is on the rise, and they are theologically conservative.[9]

Another possible reason for the charge of liberalism is the ordination of women in registered churches. In China, however, the issue is not so much a liberal/conservative one, but rather a practical one. Women have always outnumbered men in the Chinese church. Even today, the number of women believers far outstrips the men, and in the absence of male leadership, women have stepped in to fill the void. Today, at least 50 percent of registered church pastors are women. I have talked with female pastors who do not believe women should be pastors, but feel they are helping to fill a great need. It is also to be noted that the Communist government has

---

7. For the Jesus Family, see Bays, *A New History of Christianity in China*, 131–32.

8. Bays writes about the early days of the TSPM in *A New History of Christianity in China*, 160–66.

9. How, when, why, and where this transformation occurred is something that bears further study.

institutionalized the equality of men and women, so young people today assume this and have no interest in going back to a patriarchal lifestyle.

MINISTRY PROGRAMS

Most registered churches in China share a common and predictable set of ministries or programs. This includes prayer meetings, Bible studies, Sunday Schools, choirs, pre-baptism groups, community services, small groups, and youth ministries. In the large Beijing churches, Bible studies, and sometimes prayer meetings, resemble a Sunday worship service. They are attended by hundreds of people and are led by a pastor or evangelist or trained lay leader.[10] The Bible studies usually begin with several songs, after which the leader lectures (or preaches) on a passage of scripture. In many prayer meetings, personal testimonies and group prayer takes the place of the lecture. Youth services are typically well attended, and, unlike many American informal youth meetings, they are basically worship services.

Two areas of ministry require additional explanation. Often, I hear people claim that registered churches are not allowed to provide Sunday School for children or to allow children under the age of eighteen to attend the worship service. Strictly speaking, this is true as the law states that children may not be taught about Christianity (or any religion). This law, however, has been ignored by the churches for over a decade at least. Again, all one must do is observe. I have been in somewhere around one hundred churches, and almost all of them included Sunday School for children. One of my colleagues spent a good deal of her time doing Sunday School teacher training in registered churches. I have been involved in leading summer Vacation Bible School-type programs for grade school children and/or high school students through registered churches many times.

Only once were we shut down, and that was because of the special tensions surrounding the 2008 Olympics. That year we arrived in a small town in Hunan Province with a group of North American volunteers who had come to help conduct a summer camp for high school students. When we arrived, we were met at our hotel by local police who informed us that we were to remain in the hotel that night, and first thing in the morning, we were to board the bus and go back to Beijing. Unfortunately, most of

---

10. "Evangelist" is the accurate, literal translation of the Chinese word *chuandaoren*, but the people called by that name are not pastors or lay people whose job it is to go out and spread the gospel, in other words, to evangelize. Instead, *chuandaoren* are ministry interns, pastors in training. For more information about *chuandaoren*, see the following section entitled "Organization."

the volunteers were so shaken by this episode that they left for home within a couple of days. This trouble with the authorities was totally unexpected since Hunan is far from Beijing, but it became clear, first, that the government knew exactly who we were and where we were, and, second, that the government was taking no chances for trouble during the Olympics.

Children's ministry is not thriving as well as adult ministry. First, children do not usually attend regular worship services, not so much because they are not allowed, but more so that they are not encouraged. Rather, the children are expected to be in Sunday School, primarily so that they learn in an age-appropriate setting, but, more practically, because there simply is not enough room in the sanctuary. In recent years, however, I have seen more and more children in worship services. A second problem with children's ministry is the serious lack of quality material for these ministries. This is combined with ignorance on the part of leaders as to how to teach children and how to use the materials they do have. Thirdly, the lack of adequate facilities further hampers children's ministry. In the church that my wife and I attended, the entire preschool (children aged two to five) was housed in one ten by fifteen foot room. The result was bored kids packed in a tiny room with stressed teachers.

A related problem area is youth ministry. By fifth or sixth grade, older children do not want to be with the little ones in Sunday School, and most churches have nothing for them to transition into. The church we attended had a junior high program, but that was rare. By Junior High age, most kids in China are so busy with the demands of education that they have no time or energy for church activities. They can attend the youth worship service, but that is primarily for post-high school young people and often meets on a weeknight, making it difficult for younger kids to attend.

Two related areas of ministry are community service and outreach. A strictly enforced law aimed at curtailing evangelism and church visibility requires that all religious activity is restricted to church property. Churches then must get creative in finding ways to engage with their community. Some churches offer monthly free legal advice, free medical consultation, and free financial advice. Others offer free haircuts or massages. They all rely on believers to spread the word, thus giving them the opportunity to share their faith within the confines of the law.

One church is impressively innovative in this area. When I arrived in Luzhou in Sichuan Province in the summer of 2011, I saw that the Gospel Church of Luzhou now operates a hospital focused on providing quality medical care for the poor.[11] They also reach out to their community through

---

11. Yi, "Sichuan Gospel Hospital Starts."

drug education and addiction counseling programs, and on a lighter note, with song and dance performances held in public venues. While unusual, this does indicate what is possible.

Another means of outreach are the annual Christmas programs, a big deal in virtually every church. People come and wait for hours, lining up sometimes around the block in the freezing cold. Police are there in force to control traffic and crowds. The programs are something like *America's Got Talent* with many *yigong*,[12] or volunteer groups, spending weeks practicing for their specific acts. Their acts include songs, dances, drama, performances on traditional Chinese instruments, and so on. Toward the end of the program, a pastor gives a short sermon about the basics of the Christian faith, and then they tell the Christmas story.[13] Churches in larger cities often have four or five presentations of the program, some on Christmas Eve, some on Christmas day. One often needs a ticket to get in, although tickets are free. Forebodingly, in 2018, Christmas celebrations all over China were more subdued due to the heightened enforcement of government regulations.

While the Christmas programs are a sort of mass outreach, most outreach is done by individual Christians rather than by the church as an organization. Believers are taught and encouraged to make evangelism a part of their lifestyle. Their duty as Christians is to spread the good news, and the growth of the Chinese church is testament that many of them do so consistently and with a zeal that would put many Western Christians to shame.

DEMOGRAPHICS

The demographics of the church in China, both registered and unregistered, have undergone a radical transformation since the 1980s, mirroring the transformation in society as a whole. During the years preceding, during, and immediately following the Cultural Revolution (1966–76), the church in China attracted the poor, old, and rural folk. Their desperately poor churches are today filled with white haired heads, and I have preached in some of them. In one church, the sky was visible through the roof rafters, and the floor was dirt. The only restroom was a couple of square feet of dirt in an out-of-the-way corner, and coal dust covered everything. In

---

12. For *yigong*, see below under Organization.

13. A good description of a Christmas celebration is found in Selles, "Through the Narrow Gate."

these places, as younger people answered the siren call of the cities, the only people who remained were the old and the very young.[14]

In the cities, however, everything is different. The churches are filled with black haired young professionals, business people, educators, and university students. This change began in the 1980s and has accelerated in the decades since. One pastor explained that in the late 1970s and early 1980s, Christianity was still regarded as a Western religion that held no attraction for modern Chinese. But in the years following Deng Xiaoping's "reform and opening," contact with the outside world exploded. Foreign businesses began to locate in China, along with foreign personnel. Western teachers and scholars came to China by the hundreds and thousands. They brought with them new ideas and new ways of seeing the world. Perhaps most importantly, several organizations began to send droves of bright young Christians to teach English in China's universities. The influence of these organizations cannot be exaggerated. Countless numbers of university students were, and continue to be, brought to Christ through their efforts, and gradually the Chinese perception of the church has changed, and as a result, the Chinese church has changed.[15] Now Chinese young people dare to doubt Communism. The Tiananmen Square incident in June of 1989 exposed the widespread disillusionment with Communism and its heavy-handed government.[16] At the same time, people (mostly students) began to see Christianity no longer as a Western superstition, but as a legitimate worldview that provided sensible answers to their questions about life. In China, Christianity has come a long way in a short time!

ORGANIZATION

After twelve years of working with Chinese churches, I am still puzzled about how they are organized. One fact is clear: The senior pastor occupies a prominent place. As with many megachurches in other countries, registered churches in China have great respect for their senior pastors. Although their power does not match that of senior pastors in many Korean churches or that of American televangelists, their influence is still significant, albeit at the same time, limited.

---

14. ChinaSource Team, "Left-behind Children and the Rural Church."

15. These changes also led to challenges for the church and will be described in chapter 2.

16. See Vala, *The Politics of Protestant Churches*, 34–38.

Larger churches have a number of pastors and *chuandaoren,* or interns. The number of pastors is not always evenly spread from one church to another. In two similarly sized churches in Beijing, one has nine pastors and several *chuandaoren,* while the other has only three pastors and four *chuandaoren.* When I asked about this inequality, I was told that churches are free to recruit and employ their own pastors. It is something like the "calling" process of some American churches. Churches that have the funds often choose to increase their pastoral staff.

If Chinese registered churches are a mystery to the typical outside observer, Chinese seminaries are even more so. It is often difficult to tell who does what and how decisions are made. It seems that the selection of students, the content of courses, and the hiring of faculty are all openly decided by the seminary *dongshihui,* or Board of Trustees. This group is much more open than previously, when decisions were made by the seminary president and *Lianghui.* Applicants to seminary must pass a series of tests, must have leadership experience in their home church, as well as a letter of recommendation from their home pastor.[17] China has roughly twenty-five registered seminaries and Bible schools. Some only enroll students from their own province, some accept students from a few cooperating provinces, and one, Jinling Seminary in Nanjing, accepts students from anywhere in the country. Seminaries are not allowed to give out degrees that are recognized in the Chinese academic world. Once accepted to seminary, students take many of the same classes as their US counterparts, with the addition of classes like Chinese history, Chinese social issues, and Chinese politics.[18] These classes are intended to teach that patriotism is fundamental, and religious faith is secondary.[19] Most students regard these classes as a joke or a nuisance, something to be endured if one is to "do church legally" in China. I have never heard major complaints about these courses. Pastors do express concern about some aspects of seminary training. For example, seminary students are seldom, if ever, given the opportunity to preach, and they receive very little, if any, training in pastoral care. And finally, practical theology is all but ignored.

It is not clear how and where the new pastors are placed after seminary graduation. I have been told that the *Lianghui* makes all final decisions

17. Vala contends that the Three-Self Committee and the Religious Affairs Bureau control the ordination process and conduct detailed background checks on candidates. Vala, *The Politics of Protestant Churches,* 70. In my interviews and experience, however, I saw no sign of this.

18. Carsten Vala, "Protestant Reaction to the Nationalism Agenda in Contemporary China." p. 63.

19. Vala, *Politics of Protestant Churches,* 67.

about placement, but then I have also been told that students are free to look for their own matches. One pastor said that seminarians are expected, if not required, to return to their home church to serve there, and yet another said that seminarians are sent where they are most needed. It seems there is no standard procedure.

Once hired by a church, the seminary graduate becomes a *chuandaoren*. They perform all pastoral functions except for the sacraments, weddings, and the benediction. They serve as interns for a minimum of three years, and often longer. I know of *chuandaoren* who have been in that position for eight or nine years. Some *chuandaoren* choose to keep their positions as long as possible, preferring to avoid the extra responsibility and workload of full-time pastors.

In order to be ordained as pastor, the intern needs to be deemed ready for ministry by church leadership. First, aspiring pastors need to want to take this step themselves. Then he or she needs the recommendation of the senior pastor of the church they attend, as well as the approval of the informal leadership, often a group of elderly women who have influence in all church decisions. The future pastor's name and credentials are submitted to the *Lianghui* for final approval, but this step is normally a formality.

New pastors take on similar roles to what we see in the West. They preach, teach, attend meetings, and do pastoral care. I have heard people say that the pastors must attend political training sessions but those that I have talked with tell me that they have been called to do so only when a specific incident arises. Senior pastors do attend occasional meetings with government officials, but these are usually for more practical purposes such as meeting new officials, being informed of changes in government rules or practices, etc. For example, when the new religious regulations came out in 2017, all pastors had to attend training sessions put on by the *Lianghui* and the Religious Affairs Bureau. Pastors I interviewed generally agreed that no ideological pressure is applied in these meetings.

The intellectual and emotional maturity of the pastors and interns is impressively high, in spite of the fact that the job comes with less than adequate preparation and very little social status. It involves many duties and long hours with very little pay. Most urban pastors receive a few perks like an apartment and a car, but their pay is minuscule compared with that of other professionals. Pastors certainly do not go into registered church ministry for riches or recognition.

In general, the senior pastor makes all of the important decisions. This includes decisions about worship, programs, and the assigning of the various duties of the other pastors and *chuandaoren*. Typically, each staff member is in charge of a specific area or ministry. One pastor or a *chuandaoren* will be in charge of youth ministry, another of the prayer meetings, another of Bible studies, and so on. They rotate preaching. When not preaching at the main church, a pastor often preaches at various meeting points. Few churches have formal offices of deacons and even fewer have elders. Since many churches prior to the revolution had adequate elders and deacons, the present scarcity is a puzzle. At any rate, the functions of these positions seem to have been taken over by pastors, shared sometimes with an informal leadership group.

Yigong, or volunteers, play an important role in the structure and functioning of every church. A group of *yigong* might be compared to a committee or a functional small group in Western churches. There are *yigong* whose ministry is ushering, others who help with sound, others with running the bookstore, others with serving and preaching at the various *juhuidian*,[20] or meeting points, others with teaching Sunday school, and others with translation if that is offered. Some of these small groups also meet for prayer, Bible study, and support. Sometimes they also meet together as a whole for training. I have led training for *yigong* in preaching, apologetics, and various Bible books. The number of these volunteers in each church is impressive. The church we attended had about three hundred *yigong*.

The churches are offering-funded organizations. Typically, no offerings are taken during worship; instead, offering boxes are located inside and outside of the church building. Tithing, and giving in general, is taught and preached. The offerings cover church expenses and are rarely designated for anything other than the church itself. In Beijing churches, one offering is taken for Yanjing Seminary each quarter, and sometimes offerings are taken for relief in the case of a major disaster. A certain percent (usually ten) is sent on to the *Lianghui* to cover their expenses. Pastors ordained before 1982 are paid by the *Lianghui.*, but all other pastors I interviewed said they were paid by the church. Typically, church members are rarely informed about church finances, although I was in one church where a simple monthly statement of income and expenses was distributed.

Carsten Vala claims that the pastors are paid by the government. He argues that this financial arrangement is used by the TSPM to control pastors,[21] but I found no evidence of this.

I have not seen any evidence of neighboring churches working together on projects, programs or community concerns, and this is likely a matter of space constraints more than anything else. Churches can't even hold their own members, much less the members of several churches all in

---

20. For *juhuidian*, see above under "Worship."

21. Vala (2018), p. 67.

one building. One pastor told me that pastors and small groups do often get together for training and for cultural outings. Many of the Beijing churches also cosponsor a city-wide singles ministry program.

THE LIANGHUI

The relationship between the Chinese government and the registered churches remains complicated.[22] It is somewhat helpful to compare the registered churches in China to a denomination in the Western sense. Then the *Lianghui* would be equivalent to the local, regional, and national structural bodies of the church. The registered church, however, is not a denomination and the *Lianghui* is not exactly a church structure. The *Lianghui* is an organization that falls into the category of "church with Chinese characteristics." The *Lianghui* is made up of the Christian Council (CC) and the Three-Self Patriotic Movement (TSPM). Each of these groups has incarnations at the local, provincial, and national levels. So, for example, on the local level, in the city of Qingdao, the Qingdao Christian Council and the Qingdao TSPM together make up the Qingdao *Lianghui*. At the provincial level, the Shandong Province Christian Council and the Shandong Province TSPM together make up the Shandong *Lianghui*. Above that is the national *Lianghui*, with offices in Shanghai. This sounds not unlike my own denomination, the Christian Reformed Church, which has local church councils, regional classes, and a national synod, but the similarities are matched by the differences. The people who make up these organizations are not, as in my denomination, nominated from among elders and pastors at the local level, who in turn elect representatives to the next level. Rather, the personnel are chosen by the *Lianghui* at each level. The members of the CC are mostly pastors and all are Christians. The TSPM members may or may not be Christians, although most are typically local pastors. While the membership of the two bodies is mostly different, the top three or four posts in each of the two are often held by the same people.

The TSPM is a part of the government bureaucracy. Up untill recently, it answered to the State Administration of Religious Affairs (SARA), a government agency. With the new regulations, however, SARA has ceased to exist and the TSPM has been placed under the United Front Work Department (UFWD). The body with this peculiar name is part of the Communist

22. For another study of the organization of a registered church and its relation to the government, see Mark McLeister, "A Three-Self Protestant Church," in Lim, *Christianity in Contemporary China*, 234–46. He also includes a brief summary of works dealing with churches and their relationship with the government.

Party rather than the overall government. It is charged with oversight of all non-Party organizations and is known for its hardline approach. President Xi Jinping favors this agency. Most agree this does not bode well for the churches of China. One pastor said the oversight by the Communist Party's UFWD, rather than a government agency, is the most serious problem for the church in China today.

The functions of the CC and the TSPM are also different. The CC deals with "inner" church affairs, matters that apply strictly to the issues and concerns of the church. This includes the publishing of hymnals, relations with or cooperation between churches, and continuing education of pastors. The TSPM is concerned with "outer" matters such as relationships between church and State, or relations with foreign churches. In reality, the two bodies are often entangled.

On the local level, the *Lianghui* is often a thorn in the flesh of the churches. Its role is to keep a close eye on the churches. Any time a church does something slightly out of the ordinary, it needs to report this to the *Lianghui* and get its approval. At least one pastor said that his church does not bother with reports and seeking approval, while another pastor said he goes through the processes and gets his "rubber stamp." Whenever we did Vacation Bible School, for example, or summer camps at a church, the church needed to report our project to the *Lianghui* and get approval. The church also needed approval whenever I preached or taught. While the VBS and summer camps were understandably reported and approved as English Language Camps, I will never know how the church managed to get approval for my preaching and teaching, which was, strictly speaking, illegal. Likely, if I were to seek approval for these things today, I would not succeed.

On the whole, in spite of all the problems and hassles it faces, the registered churches in China are an important and thriving Christian presence in China. Hunter and Chan's description of the registered church in 1993 is worth repeating:

> As regards the Protestant church, much religious activity is conducted openly and freely. The sacraments of adult baptism and communion; preaching, prayer, and hymn-singing; Bible study and training courses; celebration of festivals; private devotion; and distribution of religious literature; all these took place in thousands of churches throughout China.[23]

---

23. Hunter and Chan, *Protestantism in Contemporary China*, 53.

2

Change and Challenges

Journal Entry, June 20, 2011, Deyang, Sichuan Province

During Sunday worship in a large, urban, registered church, I joined the congregants singing a hymn in preparation for the sermon, but I was distracted by noise and commotion in the back rows of the church. Soon people were yelling at each other and running around, and then some people were physically dragged from their seats and hauled out of the sanctuary. As ushers tried to calm things down, I asked the person next to me what was going on, and he said that the visitors were from a local cult, "recruiting" members for their movement.

Another time, a pastor described her experience in a small rural church. The members were gathered for a Bible study, and a few new people were welcomed. As the meeting progressed, the visitors began expressing new and strange ideas and proposing new interpretations of the scripture being studied. They talked about the power of the Holy Spirit, about their ability to perform miracles of various types, and about the new era that was beginning. The members were confused. All these things sounded exciting, yet somehow felt wrong. By the end of the meeting, these newcomers promised to come back next time.

CHANGE

Foreigners can barely grasp the magnitude of the changes that have occurred in both society and the church surrounding the "reform and opening" of China in the late 1970s and early 1980s. During the chaos of the Cultural Revolution (1966–76), all churches were closed. Their buildings were repurposed as factories, warehouses, and apartments. Many Christians were tortured and killed. Those who dared to meet for worship had to do so in great secrecy, in groups of a handful of believers, or in the solitude of their own homes. Christians, and any hint of a Christian church, seemed to have disappeared. There was no government agency like the Religious Affairs Bureau or the Three-Self Movement. All was swept away by Mao Zedong and the fury of his Red Guards.

Then in 1976, with the death of Mao Zedong and the rise of Deng Xiaoping, suddenly reform was in the air. The new government permitted religious expression and allowed churches to reopen. The process, of course, was not as easy as just turning a key in a lock. People were confused and skeptical. Could the new government be trusted? Was "reform" a trick to expose the Christians now in hiding? Where could Christians meet since church buildings had been repurposed during the Cultural Revolution? Who would become the new leaders? What about those who had denied their faith and colluded with the government? What exactly would be allowed and what would not? Could Christians, in good conscience, have anything to do with the government? Some of these questions, especially those related to trust, are still unanswered.

After the Cultural Revolution, Christians were not in agreement about how to proceed, and a serious rift developed between those who were determined to stay underground and others who wanted to reopen their public churches and somehow work with the ruling Communist Party. This is often marked as the beginning of the great divide between "house" churches and "government" churches. The key issue was, of course, an issue of trust. Could the government be trusted to uphold the religious freedom promised in the constitution? After all, less than twenty years before, Mao had promoted a campaign to "Let a Hundred Flowers Bloom and a Hundred Schools of Thought Contend," which first sought out critique of the government, and then ended up arresting those who criticized it. Would the same thing happen with the opening of the churches? Christians had to decide if they could put themselves within the orbit of government influence or whether they should insist on complete separation from the Communist government. The decision made by each church affected its future in profound ways.

Most unregistered church members claim that they have chosen not to trust the government because of ideology, in other words, because of the incompatibility of Christianity and Atheistic Communism. While that might certainly be one reason, the whole story is more complicated. At least since the Tang Dynasty (618–907), the government has claimed the right to shut down temples and limit the number of monks and nuns. Even when the Tang welcomed Nestorian monks and traders, their Christian message flourished only as long as the emperor was supportive. When a later emperor banned Nestorian teachings along with all foreign religions, the movement died out. Since then, Buddhism, Daoism (Taoism), Confucianism, and even Christianity have successfully contributed to Chinese culture by working carefully with the government. Professor Dan Bays, in his article "A Tradition of State Dominance," affirms that the government has always had its hands in religious affairs.

> In terms of the most fundamental level of assumptions of the state toward religion, there has hardly been a Chinese political regime from the Tang dynasty to the present that has not required a form of registration or licensing of religious groups or has not assumed the right to monitor and intervene in religious affairs.[1]

In the 1980s, as churches slowly reopened, those who chose to work within the reestablished Three-Self Patriotic Movement and Religious Affairs Bureau, were the minority.[2] Their numbers and their presence, however, increased at an astonishing pace. Most crucial was the change of their image as an old, rural, uneducated church to that of a young, urban, professional church. One pastor explained that prior to reform and opening, most Chinese had a negative view of Christianity as having no real connection with their daily lives. It was associated with foreigners, always something to be suspicious of. In contrast, starting especially in the 1990s, a new generation of young people, restless for change, saw something in the demeanor of Christians that has made them curious and open to hearing the Christian message. According to this pastor, being a Christian was no longer foreign or weird, but instead attractive.

Westerners typically hear that unregistered churches refuse to cooperate with registered churches and that registered churches are controlled by the government. For pastors of registered churches, however, neither the

---

1. See Daniel Bays, "A Tradition of State Dominance," in *God and Caesar in China*, edited by Kindop, 26.

2. The estimates I have seen and heard generally posit that two-thirds of China's Christians are in unregistered churches.

government nor unregistered churches loom large in their everyday life and ministry, and when I interviewed pastors about the challenges they faced, no one mentioned either the government or unregistered churches. They are concerned with the stuff of daily ministry: Bible study, prayer, worship, counseling, etc. For the most part, they minimize contact with the government, and unregistered churches seldom show up on their radar.

CULTS

Both in Beijing and in the other churches I visited throughout China, pastors gave me the same answer when asked about the problems they face: the number one challenge is cults. A few registered church pastors claim that any unregistered church group is a cult, but the term more accurately applies to a religious sect that notably aggrandizes its leader, who is self-serving and usually has a political agenda. The Chinese have two commonly used words to identify these groups. While largely interchangeable in normal speech, *xiejiao* refers to heretical teaching, while *yiduan* refers to the group of people who follow the heretical teaching. Whichever word is used, Christian church pastors view these groups and their teachings as heretical and their behavior disruptive.

Consider this story that appeared in *ChinaSource*:

> On May 12, 2019, Xiao Qing, a Christian woman, encountered five or six people who claimed to be Christians after attending a Sunday worship service. Distributing gospel tracts to passers-by, these men fervently asked for her contact information and invited her to visit their "church." After some discussion, Xiao Qing felt something was off. These men only shared from the book of Revelation, said nothing about Jesus, and made vague statements about their church. Afterward, she searched online and found that their tracts were the same as those of the Korean *Shincheonji*, the "New Heaven and New Earth" sect.[3]

These heterodox sects have been part of the Chinese landscape seemingly forever. Some are offshoots of Christianity,[4] while many others find their origin in Buddhism, Daoism, or folk religion. All are persistent. Their disciples really do interrupt worship services and at times, they do drag Christians out of their pews to get them outside to intimidate them. At the

---

3. ChinaSource Team, "Cult Activity in China Impacts Churches."

4. For a brief but excellent description of some of the heterodox sects of Christian origin, see Bays, *A New History of Christianity in China*, 195–97.

very least, members stand near entrances and accost people as they enter or leave church. These groups have often provided the ideology and manpower for dynastic change. Two fairly recent examples are the *Taiping Tianguo* (the Heavenly Kingdom of Great Peace) and the Boxers.[5] The *Taiping* had Christian connections while the Boxers were vehemently anti-Christian but still religious. Both played a role in the demise of the Qing Dynasty (1644–1911). In fact, heterodox sects of one type or another have been a significant factor in the rise and fall of many dynasties, and any new government has ample historical reason to be suspicious of any movement resembling a cult.

The government recognizes only five religions: Buddhism, Daoism, Islam, Protestantism, and Catholicism. All other religions are banned. This includes any unregistered Christian churches or heterodox groups that rise up and provoke the government. One of the great ironies of religious life in China is that while the constitution supposedly allows and protects religious freedom, that freedom is circumscribed when the government deems a religion to pose a threat to the status quo. Thus, the officially atheistic communist government finds itself trying to figure out which religions are orthodox and which are heterodox.

How do they decide? What criteria do they use? Why do they do this? At times, decisions to curtail or restrict church activity are political. A government official, for example, may want to move up in the ranks, and being either strict or lenient with the local Christian church may help him attain his goal. I have heard several pastors say that in the case of the removal of crosses from churches in Wenzhou, the reason was attributed to a local official trying to enhance his resume.

At other times, government officials have a need for discernment in deciding which religious groups are contributing to community stability and which are destabilizing. This, then, can lead to cooperation between church and State. In some instances, local officials work with local church leaders to make decisions about a particular group's legitimacy. A pastor in a rural community told me this story. She was given the assignment (she saw it as a call from God) of starting a new church in an area where Christianity was growing rapidly but there were no churches, only meeting points or "*juhuidian.*" This rural area was also home to many heterodox sects, and the local officials were at a loss about dealing with the influence that these groups were having on the community's cohesiveness and morale. Many of the citizens knew little or nothing about Christianity, and the sects were yet another mystery. In order to decide which leaders were to be encouraged

---

5. For the Taiping, see Spence, *God's Chinese Son*. For the Boxers, see Esherick, *The Origins of the Boxer Uprising*.

and which silenced, the town officials (all Communist Party members) asked the pastor to teach them about Christianity. They all gathered at the church for a special meeting and listened to the pastor describe the basic doctrines of Christianity. Thus, the Party officials heard the gospel and the grace of God! When Christmas came, so did the group of officials. There they were, in the front several rows, listening again to the gospel. Later, one of the officials told the pastor that if he ran across someone who claimed to be a Christian, he would know that person was okay if he attended her church. The lesson? Sometimes government involvement does not necessarily mean government oppression. Sometimes the two can cooperate for mutual benefit.

This story gives rise to other questions. Why should the government be involved at all, whether dealing with a church or a heterodox sect? What about the non-cultic unregistered Christian churches in the area? Is the church in the story compromising its beliefs by cooperating in this way? These questions remain difficult. For now, it bears repeating that not every meeting between government officials and church leaders is a case of the government oppressing the church or the church blindly following the government.

Chinese pastors often refer to areas where cults are proliferating as *hunluan*, meaning confused, messed up, and chaotic. In China, the State has always been the provider and protector of social stability, at least in theory, and that is still the case today. This is exemplified by the ubiquitous signs and banners promoting *hexie*, or harmony, that one sees all over Beijing. The Protestant church in China, in reality, has a much more difficult time functioning in places that are *hunluan*, than it does in communities that have a climate of *hexie*. Most registered churches are willing, therefore, to put up with light restrictions on their activities if they can then count on the government's heavy-handed restrictions on what they see as cult activity.

THE SEVENTH DAY ADVENTIST CHURCH

Nothing is clean-cut in China, or as a friend of mine likes to say, in China nothing is as it seems. Even though the government officially recognizes only five legitimate religions, two other denominations are tolerated as well. First, the Orthodox Church has a ministry in China. This church does not have an impact on the registered churches, and I know little of their story. The Seventh Day Adventist Church (SDA) is the other accepted religious organization, and it occupies a unique position in China. While in Western cultures, the SDA is considered at least a quasi-legitimate Protestant church, in China the registered churches regard the SDA as a full-fledged cult. One pastor showed me some recent pamphlets from the SDA that, among other heterodox teachings, gave a precise date for the end of the world and Christ's return. In contrast, however, the government does not view the SDA as a heterodox religious group, but rather as an "organization" of sorts. They do not pressure them to register as a church, and they find no reason to harass them. The SDA exists, it seems, quite happily outside of the system. None of the people I asked about the SDA knew exactly how to explain this.

This would not be of much concern for the registered churches, except that the government often declares that SDA congregations can use the facilities of the registered churches, most often, of course, on Saturday, the SDA Sabbath. Unfortunately, it is not uncommon for SDA congregations to wield their entitled status and demand use of the facilities during the week as well. This has led to conflicts. Once on a Monday, when I was running a Vacation Bible School in a registered church, SDA members came and demanded that we vacate so they could hold a meeting. When church pastors refused, they were physically attacked by the SDA members.

SHORTAGE OF PASTORS AND BIBLICAL SCHOLARS

Another area of concern is the lack of leaders. The phenomena of rapid growth and widespread appeal of Christianity in China has led to a crisis of supply and demand. Both pastors and Biblical scholars are in short supply. Almost every pastor identifies this as a crucial concern. Just a few examples will suffice. In Beijing and other cities, the registered churches are few and large. The church we attended averages five thousand to six thousand worshipers on Sunday, yet it had only three pastors and four *chuandaoren,* or interns. That is one pastor for almost one thousand parishioners. Other churches are similar or have an even worse ratio. How does one do any kind of meaningful ministry under such circumstances? Small town churches are understaffed as well. One church I know of has just one pastor who ministers to almost one thousand members, along with overseeing more than twenty churches that he has planted in surrounding rural areas. Registered churches also lack accomplished musicians, and those who understand the relationship between music and biblical theology are virtually nonexistent. Many congregations have no pastor at all. I know of two pastors who farm on the side just to make ends meet. Doubtless there are many, many more like them.

Other reasons for the shortage are that pastors' social standing is low, the requirements for ordination are almost overwhelming, and the pay is poor. Add to these the huge workload, which often leads to burnout. According to one pastor, the problem is far from being solved, and adding to the problem is the decreasing number of seminary students. In Beijing, many seminary students used to come straight from high school, saving them considerable time and money. Currently, seminary applicants are required to have a college degree, and the number of people who are willing to put in this much time in school for a position with such low pay and status is understandably small. Additionally, the government limits the number of students allowed to enroll in seminaries, hoping, I suppose, that by limiting the number of pastors, they can limit the number of Christians. The miracle is that there are not even fewer pastors.

The number of Biblical scholars and teachers is also low. China's seminaries do not have advanced degree programs. In fact, they do not give out any degrees at all. In the past, some pastors or students have gone to a foreign seminary, but found that when they got back to China, the *Lianghui* would not allow them to serve in the registered churches. This has begun to change. In the last few years, some churches send their own students abroad for further study, but this, too, has challenges. Not only is the cost of foreign study high, but more seriously, few Chinese students have sufficient English skills to succeed at a foreign seminary. Equally, few Western seminaries have professors who can teach in Chinese. Now, Christians fear that new regulations could further hamper the ability of pastors to study in foreign seminaries.

Related to the shortage of biblical scholars and pastors is a low level of biblical theological knowledge among lay people. Many Christians attend a church and receive their spiritual teaching from a pastor who has had little, if any, formal training. Since their own level of spiritual formation is so low, they are often unable to share their faith at deep levels, and unable to resist the arguments of sect members who attempt to lead them in unorthodox directions. These believers know Bible stories and individual passages well, often able to recite long passages from memory, but lack any meaningful understanding of what the Bible teaches as a whole or how the entire Bible fits together.

A special concern is the need for better, meaningful pastoral care. Virtually all of the pastors interviewed put this near the top of the challenges faced by the church. Pastoral care requires a significant investment of time and training, both of which are in short supply or nonexistent. Most pastors hope that pastoral care will be administered by *yigong* (volunteer workers), or through small groups; unfortunately, most members of these groups are not prepared to do so.

The challenges of premarital counseling are particularly pressing. Not only do pastors have little time for this, and, more importantly, lack adequate training, but also Chinese culture presents its own roadblocks. In Chinese culture, marriage has always been strictly a family affair. What happens in a marriage stays in that marriage; it is no one else's business. This attitude has often resulted in simmering bitterness in the home. Traditionally, Chinese husbands could punish their wives in any way they saw fit, including capital punishment, for what we would consider minor infractions. Of course, the laws have changed, but many of the attitudes remain. Add to this a growing economic prosperity that can give rise to many conflicts, especially over money. Also, many young Chinese have bought into the Western practice of living together before or without marriage. China does not have a well-established social services network, so a church pastor would likely be the only resource for a couple seeking support and guidance. All of these things are mixed together and thrown into the lap of an ill-prepared pastor or *chuandaoren*. What are they to do? They have not had a single class in pastoral care, much less one that is focused on marital and premarital counseling. Some of them, especially *chuandaoren*, are not married, so they have no personal experience of marriage and often have little experience of life in general. Of course, everyone acknowledges that the churches should be a source of counsel and support for its members, but given the circumstances, it will be a long road.

One lay member, commenting on pastoral leadership and pastoral care, described her church of the last ten years as stagnant. She noted that the church does not provide in-depth training in spiritual growth and discipleship. Because of this, people are switching to unregistered churches. Another argued that worship in the registered churches is simply a matter of going through the motions; there is no real spiritual growth. One pastor pointed out that the church needs to figure out how to keep youth from leaving the church. Once again, given the crushing level and variety of needs faced by pastors and other church leadership, it is surprising that more pastors do not burn out.

Another hardship faced by pastors and lay people alike is a feeling of isolation. In most places in the world, pastors and Christians in general can and do get together with Christians from different churches and places. These opportunities are a source of spiritual encouragement and mutual understanding. Once, I participated in taking a group of pastors to the United States for a worship symposium. Many of the pastors were not functional in English and could understand very little of what was being said, but that was not a serious deterrent for them. They were more interested in observing and interacting with Christians from other places and backgrounds. They appreciated experiencing the fact that they were not alone and that there were many people from all over the world praying for them.

RISING EXPECTATIONS

While some members are satisfied with the status quo, others, especially younger members, are restless for change. One pastor said that his parishioners more often question what he preaches. This pastor said that young people think differently and have different needs that the pastors find challenging to meet. In spite of China's infamous information firewall, people in China now have access to the bigger world through the internet, especially if they have a Virtual Private Network (VPN). They can now watch any of a thousand worship services online, and inevitably, they compare and find their own worship services wanting. Seeing vital and exciting worship online, many people wonder why theirs is so dry and old fashioned. I have heard many complaints about sermons that seemed irrelevant, failing to address the issues of real, everyday living. I have also been told that most sermons are so long that they have a numbing effect.

One result of this restlessness is the rise of that quintessentially American phenomenon, "church-hopping." And, of course, the church hoppers are not only sampling other registered churches; they are also going down the street to the unregistered churches and often finding worship that is moving and meaningful and sermons that touch their hearts. I don't mean to say that all house churches offer this type of worship, but enough do, and the word gets out about them. Many unregistered churches provide exciting and active youth ministry. Young people might first hear about Jesus and be converted and baptized in a registered church, only to transition to an unregistered church after a few years.

Large registered churches typically offer Bible studies and prayer meetings in mass gatherings. While these may do a fair job of disseminating information, they fail miserably in providing a safe environment for sharing one's personal faith and challenges.[6] Yet that is exactly what members are longing for. In cities with large populations (twenty-one million in Beijing), anonymity and loneliness are the order of the day, and young people especially are on the search for relationships, for friendships, for a sense

---

6. One exception is small group prayer time in the large prayer meetings.

of belonging, for people they can trust, for intimacy. Vala points out that, ironically, the longing for intimacy is leading people to leave the church:

> Interviews also showed that young Chinese Protestants leave official churches in Beijing and Nanjing due to uninspiring preaching, a paucity of activities, or the lack of intimacy in the congregations. As a consequence, although the values proclaimed from the pulpits of official churches resemble those of unregistered congregations, the practices differ, and therefore many Protestants develop a weak sense of belonging and some of them leave official churches altogether.[7]

Small group ministry is vital to any church, and the registered churches in China are learning to lean on them more and more as a form of pastoral care. In many large churches, members have taken things into their own hands and have formed extensive small group communities within the church. Some form groups around the functions they perform (ushers, communion servers, etc.), other form prayer groups, or study groups, or even hobby centered groups. Some of these groups meet in the church facilities and others in homes. Across the street from the church we attended, there used to be a KFC restaurant. If you looked in the windows after church, you would see multiple small groups studying the Bible or praying. Sadly, about five years ago, the restaurant was closed for unspecified reasons.

STILL MORE CHALLENGES

Some critics of registered churches scoff at the idea of registered churches having financial problems since they get money and other help from the government, but according to the pastors I spoke with, the churches are actually self-funded. A rare exception to this is when the government contributes funds toward acquiring land or buildings. But even in these cases, the land or buildings at stake originally belonged to the church before the Cultural Revolution, and the government is simply aiding the church in recovering what was theirs. In recent years, some government initiatives have inadvertently threatened the financial stability of these churches. The government has been moving people out of cities like Beijing, many of whom were part of a church. The loss of their membership and their offerings has impacted the ministry of the churches they were forced to leave.

---

7. Vala, *Politics of Protestant Churches,* 112.

Many churches are responding to the drop in numbers by emphasizing evangelism, although they note that people are not as enthusiastic about spreading the gospel as they used to be. Some have placed the focus on encouraging believers to evangelize their own families. Others focus, instead, on deepening people's faith. One pastor said that his church's ministry has shifted towards social action,[8] and they spend their resources establishing nursing homes and orphanages.

Finally, rural areas are in serious decline. Young people are moving to the cities, leaving the old people, and the old ways, and the old churches behind.

IDENTITY CRISIS

One pastor said, insightfully, that the church in China is experiencing an identity crisis. She noted that since the 1930s, the Christian church in China was weak and without social influence. Recently, however, even though the church has grown numerically, its social influence has not kept pace. The modern Chinese church is lost and wandering, wondering how and where it fits in its society. It also wonders how to confront growing materialism and changing lifestyle mores. According to Brent Fulton of *ChinaSource*, churches are too busy with internal church issues to even have a sound understanding of their role in modern Chinese society.[9] He had in mind especially unregistered churches, but in the registered churches, this busyness is compounded by the reality that churches are forbidden by the government to do any ministry off of their property. It is hard to build and maintain a meaningful social role and identity under these circumstances.

Although some churches have seen a decline in membership, the sheer number of Christians is still problematic for the churches. Structurally and in terms of personnel, the churches are equipped to handle about a quarter of the number of believers that flock to them each Sunday (as well as weekdays). Too many Christians! It is a nice problem to have, but it is still a problem.

---

8. See chapter 1 for the ways churches are becoming more involved in social action.

9. Fulton, *China's Urban Christians*, 116–17.

BACK TO THE SEMINARIES

Completing the circle, most of these challenges point back to the training of leaders, in short, to the seminaries. With the low pay and social standing, added to the heavy workload, recruiting sufficient numbers of seminary students remains difficult. Most of the pastors, nevertheless, were positive and hopeful. They see strong faith commitments in a new generation of professors at the seminaries who are working to make the seminary experience more relevant, more complete. Professors are now hired by a board of trustees rather than by the seminary president, and this is leading to a higher level of quality.[10] Some seminaries are experimenting with new venues like correspondence courses, off-campus workshops and seminars, and even one-year on-campus courses that are focused on the basics.

Problems remain. I heard from several people that seminary graduates feel ill-prepared to preach or to do pastoral care. One Beijing pastor, speaking about Yanjing Seminary in Beijing, lamented that not only is the number of students entering seminary too small, but also their educational background and their *suzhi*, or knowledge of proper character and behavior, is too low. This is a hard problem for the seminary to solve, but, on the whole, I heard more positive than negative assessments. Listen to a Yanjing Seminary professor talk about the seminary:

> Does Yanjing Seminary adequately prepare students for ministry? No seminary can do that. But we give students a foundation. We try to mold students into having a biblical foundation concerning discipline and style of life. We also try to cover the basic tasks of ministry: preaching, sacraments, worship leading, and the basics of pastoral care. We try to help students make the transition to ministry. They need to know how to use the scripture in their time and place. We try to equip students to communicate effectively with people from all walks of life. Our seminary provides students with a good foundation.

RELEVANCY

The overarching challenge, of course, is for the registered churches to remain relevant. For so many years, the Chinese church was poor, old, and uneducated. Now the church faces those who have more education than anyone

---

10. One pastor said that professors were appointed by the Religious Affairs Bureau, but he was the only one who said this.

on the church staff, those who are experts at reading trends in fashion and in the marketplace. As China becomes more and more affluent, the church is also struggling more and more with materialism and consumerism. As in so many other modernized countries, the church does not compete well with the mall. Parishioners, especially young members, are struggling with changing morals and lifestyles. Society's sexual attitudes have changed; mistresses are common and prostitution is ubiquitous; divorce rates are soaring; cheating and corruption seem to be everywhere. Parents pressure their children to pursue what they did not have: money, power, and success.[11] The internet has now connected China to the whole world, and young Chinese, in particular, see themselves as part of a global economy and culture. How does Christianity remain relevant both in church and in society? How can the church compete with the mall and the night clubs? This challenge needs to be addressed, and I propose that it may be the key to all the others.

11. See Vala, *Politics of Protestant Churches*, 99–101.

3

Church-State Relations—Who's in Charge?

Journal Entry, June 26, 2011, Ankang, Sichuan Province

Finding the Ankang Church was a challenge. I flagged down a taxi near the hotel and the driver said he knew the address, but when we arrived, there was no church. The taxi driver told me to get out and ask someone else. I found an old couple who said the church had moved, and they gave me general directions to the new location. It didn't seem too far, so I set out on foot. When I got to about the halfway point, I stopped and asked a shopkeeper, and she gave me clear directions—to what turned out to be the Catholic Church. I figured that the Catholics would know the location of their competition, and sure enough, the fellow in the church office gave me directions, saying it was no more than a ten-minute walk. His directions took me along a river down a road under construction. After walking ten, then fifteen, and then twenty minutes, I still saw no church. Finally, I asked a young man on a bike. He said I had come too far, and I needed to turn around and go to the first intersection and turn left. He said I would find the church under construction there. I followed his directions and indeed found a church under construction. The picture of the planned final product looked impressive, but they were only as far as the foundation. Several workers there tried to direct me to yet another location, but their proficiency in Putonghua (standard Mandarin dialect) was questionable, and I understood little of what they said. Eventually, one of them pointed to yet another location. As I walked on, a man came up behind me and said, "Thanks be to God." It turned out to be an evangelist at the church, and he offered to walk me to the church. We walked down several streets and alleys and finally came to an unmarked courtyard. No sign, no cross, no indication of what sort of place this might be. Just a courtyard full of laundry hanging out to dry, discarded furniture, and assorted rubble, surrounded by buildings that looked ready to topple over (and in some cases already had). Here I was escorted into a large garage/warehouse sort of room adjacent to the makeshift sanctuary. I was cordially welcomed by the church's two pastors, Pastor Li and his wife, Pastor Ren. We sat down in couches in a mostly empty garage that I feared would come tumbling down around us at any minute, and we had a great talk.

Pastor Li and Pastor Ren, had been at the church since 1990, following their graduation from the Shaanxi Bible School. The church had been started in 1889 by missionaries from the China Inland Mission, but in 1899, a missionary from Norway replaced the original missionaries and he reestablished the church as what Pastor Li called a Lutheran/Presbyterian hybrid. This church is not currently growing. About three hundred of their one thousand members gather for the one worship service on Sundays. The others attend meeting points in the neighboring area, while many do not attend because of work schedules, family obligations, etc. The majority of congregants are elderly. Baptism, held once a year, brings in about twenty new members. The church offers the usual prayer services, Bible studies, and Sunday School, but the temporary quarters make things understandably difficult. They are hoping to start a youth group, but lack leadership and facilities. They are eagerly looking forward to the completion of the new building, hopefully by Easter. The new church will seat about one thousand five hundred.

When asked about the challenges facing the church, Pastor Li launched into an impassioned speech about division amongst churches. He blamed many house church members for labeling the registered churches as Three-Self. He noted that the Three-Self is not a church, but just an organization. The church is the body of believers who belong to Christ. He also said that being a true church does not depend on where someone worships, but rather on their relationship with God, their understanding of scripture, and the orthodoxy of their beliefs. He was concerned about the tendency of many house churches toward heretical beliefs. He laid on all pastors the responsibility for reaching out, acknowledging that the powers of darkness are great, and that many temptations in contemporary society lure young people down an evil path. At the same time, he described this as the "golden age of the church in China," citing the phenomenal growth that has occurred all over the country.

This church struggles financially. Only about half of the money for the new building has been raised so far. Pastor Li gave me a copy of a letter that had been sent to all the churches in China, soliciting financial help, and he made it clear that whatever help I could give would be appreciated.

I decided to stay one more night in Ankang and attend church there Sunday morning. There were about three hundred in attendance at the 8:30 service. Shortly after I arrived, Pastor Ren motioned for me to join her outside. There she explained to me that she had asked the evangelist who was preaching (Pastor Li had duties at another church) to cut her sermon short so I would have time to "share." I protested that my Chinese was poor, and I had not prepared for this, but after continued pleading on her part, I agreed to speak for a few minutes. As promised, the preacher cut her sermon short, ending it at one hour and fifteen minutes. It was a pretty good sermon on sin and our need to repent, but since she didn't say much about God's promise to forgive, I decided to focus on that. It was my first attempt at "preaching" without any preparation or manuscript, and to my surprise, I spoke for fifteen minutes, and the congregation seemed accepting and appreciative. At the end of the service, it was my pleasure to give the blessing in English and Chinese.

A COMPLICATED RELATIONSHIP

The relationship between the Christian Church, the Communist Party, and the official government of China is an unusual one, counterintuitive to Westerners, and something that even the Chinese struggle to define. In 1946 Mao Zedong railed against Christianity, labeling it the opiate of the people and declaring that it was bound for destruction. From all appearances, during the dark days of his Cultural Revolution, he seemed to have succeeded in bringing about its destruction. As Carsten Vala explains in his recent book, *The Politics of Protestant Churches and the Party-State in China: God Above Party?*, during the Mao era (1949–76),[1] the State almost completely dismantled the churches by using tactics like the Denunciation

---

1. Vala, *Politics of Protestant Churches,* 28–31.

Campaign (brutally criticizing friends and coworkers), complete closing of churches, and "marrying force to ideology."[2]

The situation changed following the death of Mao Zedong in 1976. His successor, Deng Xiaoping, initiated a program of "reform and open- ing," which included the government's new attempt to accommodate and control religion rather than to stamp it out.[3] In spite of this more genial approach, the government's goal remained one of, "winning over religious leaders, promoting Chinese Communist Party-focused patriotism among millions of Protestants under Three-Self Patriotic Movement oversight, and urging Protestants to 'adapt' Christianity to the Party line."[4] Over the next fifty years, the Communist Government, firmly atheist at its core, vacillated between severe retribution toward aggressive church groups and passive tolerance toward others. Leading Chinese religion scholar Fenggang Yang helpfully identifies four distinct periods of government policy towards churches from 1949 to 2009:

> Chronologically [the regulation of religion] has had four dis-
> tinct periods: (1) from 1949 to 1957, the Party-state suppressed
> various religions and co-opted the five major religions through
> establishing the "patriotic" religious associations; (2) from
> 1957 to 1966 the socialist transformation was imposed to the
> "patriotic" religious groups and forcefully reduced the number
> of religious venues; (3) from 1966 to 1979, all religious venues
> were closed down, and religion was banned; (4) from 1979 to
> 2009, limited tolerance of certain religious groups was governed
> by increasingly restrictive regulations.[5]

Yang points out that while there have been drastic reforms in the economy, religious policy has remained stagnant and ideology driven.[6]

Carsten Vala outlined another helpful way to look at the relationship of church and State over the last fifty years, arguing that while the State at- tempted domination over the churches, the churches responded in kind by negotiating for more manageable scenarios. This domination-negotiation paradigm, Vala argues, is more accurate than the domination-resistance model proposed by previous scholars. He begins by identifying the funda- mental tension between church and State. Looking at church/State relations from 1949 till the present, he says:

2. Vala, *Politics of Protestant Churches*, 31.

3. Vala, *Politics of Protestant Churches*, 32.

4. Vala, *Politics of Protestant Churches*, 41.

5. Yang, *Religion in China*, 65.

6. Yang, *Religion in China*, 65.

My domination-negotiation perspective builds upon the earlier scholarship on the tense and coercive nature of regime-religion relations to acknowledge that the Chinese Communist Party still asserts undisputed authority to set the limits on religious practices. Further, this perspective recognizes that coercive domination is still a fact for religious believers who refuse any communication with the state.[7]

Yang Fenggang further describes State-church relationships as being affected over time by three different philosophical approaches with which the Communist government has experimented and the sort of government policies that have accompanied them. He labels the various approaches:

> *Militant atheism* leads to anti-religious measures, *enlightenment atheism* serves as the theoretical basis for a limited tolerance of religion while insisting on atheist propaganda, and *mild atheism* justifies an even greater tolerance of religion.[8]

The Communist government of China is an atheist regime committed to controlling and restricting religious expression in China. At any given time, Christians must gauge their government's current degree of tolerance or intolerance, and tiptoe as best they can. While I was in China from 2006–2017, the government seemed to be dealing with the churches from what Yang Fenggang would identify as an enlightened atheist or even a mild atheist posture, but since I left China, the government seems to be swinging back to what he characterizes as a more militantly atheist posture.

THE ROLE OF THE LIANGHUI

In 1951, an agency was established to register and keep account of all churches. The agency is called the *Lianghui*, which, roughly translated, means "two councils" or "two committees." The two councils are the Three-Self Patriotic Movement (TSPM) and the Christian Council (CC). While the Christian Council is concerned more with internal church issues, the TSPM focuses more on external affairs. Because it relates directly with the government, the TSPM gets most of the attention and criticism. The churches belonging to the *Lianghui* are commonly referred to as Three-Self churches, a negative identifying marker implying that the Three-Self churches are completely controlled by the government.

7. Vala, *Politics of Protestant Churches*, 10.

8. Yang, *Religion in China*, 46.

Registered church leaders have to live with the name, but they refuse to acknowledge that the TSPM controls them. For them, the TSPM refers not to a dominating structure, but rather to a bridge-like structure between the church and the government. The truth is, however, the TSPM is more complicated than a simple bridge-like organization. When I asked specifically what the TSPM does, most pastors and lay people used words like "be responsible for," "manage," or most often "*guanli*" meaning "to oversee." One pastor said the churches "are under the supervision of the TSPM." At the same time, these same pastors insist that the churches do what they want and are not controlled by the government. Maybe it is simply a matter of semantics or maybe a case of "socialism with Chinese characteristics." Maybe it is actually oversight without control, much the way Vala describes domination-negotiation.[9]

DOMINATION-NEGOTIATION

To their credit, the registered churches have been impressively adept at managing much of the imposition of the State by strategically tempering the domination stance of the government through initiated negotiation. While they publicly defer to the domination role of the State, they find within the structure an ability to negotiate and even wield influence. Vala describes it this way:

> Negotiation continues to be at play between Protestants and the Party-state under the image of domination, for several reasons. First, the Party-state is less omnipresent than domination perspectives suggest, as its agents devolve administrative responsibility to Protestant association [TSPM and CC] officials. Second, the Protestant associations themselves act in a domination mode only part of the time, under specific conditions, most often when Religious Affairs Bureau (RAB) cadres are physically present or when they install loyalists [those who support the government] as Protestant officials. Third, domination can be more apparent than real.[10]

Vala notes that out of necessity, the behavior of Protestant leaders does not always conform to their words, especially if they are being closely watched. He affirms that, "in calling it an image of domination, I am trying

9. See Vala, *Politics of Protestant Churches*, 11–15.

10. Vala, *Politics of Protestant Churches*, 200.

to point to the idea that much of its foundation lies in fiction rather than fact."[11]

To put it yet another way, while the TSPM gives the government access to church activity, it also gives the churches access to government activity. The *Lianghui* does have a part in things like admission to seminary, ordination of pastors, approval of any unusual programs or activities, and education regarding government rules and regulations. But conversely, anything that the government is doing comes to the churches through the TSPM. At times, a TSPM member will contact a senior pastor, or the government will sponsor full-fledged meetings or classes. While these meetings are often regarded as a nuisance by the pastors, they can also be helpful. One pastor said, "When you are a pastor, you are recognized and expected to be a leader in society as well. So, there are classes to familiarize you with contemporary society." In all of my discussion about these State/church meetings, none seem to have been initiated with accompanying threats or force. It is also worth noting that most of the *Lianghui* members are also local pastors.

Vala further posits that a factor attributing to the rise of the domination-negotiation strategy within the *Lianghui* has to do with a personnel shortage in the State Administration of Religious Affairs (SARA) and the other bureaus that have responsibility for religious affairs. As the number of Christians increased rapidly, especially in the 1980s and 1990s, many more trained State workers were needed to "oversee" all of these new Christians. These, however, proved hard to come by. Pay and prestige were low, the ratio of Christians to government personnel could go as high as ten thousand to one, and the opportunities for advancement were few.[12] As a result, because the State knows it does not have the resources for heavy-handed enforcement, it uses its rather limited resources for negotiated enforcement. Churches are required to regularly work with, hopefully via negotiation, their *Minzongban*, the local government agency that is responsible for everyday activities in its neighborhood. The church needs to get approval from this agency whenever something they do will impact the neighborhood. For example, when the church plans its Christmas activities, it needs to work in tandem with the *Minzongban* to control traffic and crowds and keep order. This sort of mutual cooperation often strengthens relations between church and State and encourages negotiation.

It is important to remember that the State's default approach is still domination, and, in the last decade, the church has seen an alarming swing away from negotiation and toward more domination. A couple of examples

11. Vala, *Politics of Protestant Churches,* 200.

12. Vala, *Politics of Protestant Churches,* 41–44.

illustrate this. Many people have heard about the tearing down of church crosses in and around Wenzhou. Although most Westerners saw this as a clear-cut case of government persecution, several pastors and lay people blamed the churches as much as the government. They said the crosses did violate building codes and therefore should have been torn down for safety reasons. Others claim, however, that the crosses were torn down because a local official hated Christianity and wanted to further his career. Which is it? It's not always easy to tell.

The other example of government pressure has to do with English-language worship services in Beijing. As of about 2012, three registered churches in the Beijing area held English language worship services. One of these services hosted about one thousand attendees, the other two, one hundred or less. In late 2017 the government closed down the two largest services, leaving only the smallest one open. I had been preaching twice a month at one of the small churches, which had experienced serious pressure because I was a foreigner, and that is probably why the service was finally shut down. The largest service was likely shut down because it attracted too many people. The one remaining English language church has stayed open, and its pastor says that he doubts that it was the government that shut down the other churches. As for his service being able to continue, he claims that, "it is purely God's grace."

Communication between church and government can go both ways. While the churches can make their concerns known to the government through the TSPM, I had the impression that they seldom did. In general, the pastors' view of the TSPM was that it was best avoided if possible. One pastor commented, "Our church follows the rules and regulations about classes and studying, but there is little contact with the government otherwise; we do not seek it out." Another said, "The church does not involve itself with government issues."

The other half of the *Lianghui*, the Christian Council, seems to be less visible but more appreciated. The Christian Council (which, like the TSPM, has local, provincial, and national incarnations) is concerned with the spiritual aspects of churches. Mostly, its role is to oversee pastoral training, teaching, preaching, and administering of the sacraments. It also arranges for continuing education for pastors and church development.

A common belief is that the government appoints the members of the *Lianghui* and those members are not even Christians. Sometimes the State Administration for Religious Affairs (SARA), an oversight agency of the Chinese government, appoints a TSPM member, but most of the members are appointed by TSPM members and are local senior pastors or seminary professors and are definitely Christians. On the provincial level, members are chosen from among the local committees while national members are chosen from the provincial level. The top several positions in each body are generally held by the same people, assuring that the two organizations will be working closely with each other.

In 2019, a major government restructuring of religious oversight bodes poorly for the future of the *Lianghui*. SARA was dismantled, and the *Lianghui* was put under the supervision of a Communist Party agency, the United Front Work Department. This means that they are under the Party, not the government. For those who come from a background that emphasizes separation of church and State, this is hard to comprehend. How is a church both a church and part of the government bureaucracy? For Chinese Christians who come from a tradition in which opposites are frequently held in tension, it's not quite so difficult.

Part of the reason for misunderstanding between the registered church and Western Christians, not to mention the strained relations with Chinese unregistered church members, is that people tend to assume that the registered churches are fully supportive of the government. Following the shutdown of Xian Church in Beijing in 2018, an unregistered church leader said to me, with a good deal of anger and hurt in her voice, "Why don't registered churches help us out and influence the government on our behalf?" This sort of question belies a misunderstanding of the registered church and its relationship with the government. The registered churches that I am familiar with are not friends of the government or the Party. Quite the opposite, the registered churches put up with more government meddling and regulations than most of the unregistered churches. It could be argued that from 1990 until 2015, the unregistered churches were more free than their registered counterparts. They could, and still often can, go about their ministry with little interference from the government. The contention that the registered churches are in bed with the government is for the most part simply wrong. It would be beneficial for all churches to realize that the problem is not other churches, but the threat that the government poses and will always pose to Christianity in an atheist Communist regime.

LISTENING TO THE PASTORS

Is it possible to negotiate and compromise with this government? Registered and unregistered churches obviously have different answers to that question. Unregistered churches seem to believe that the current government is so anti-Christian that compromise would be a betrayal of their faith.

Different unregistered churches answer this question differently, but they all seem to agree, by either words or actions or both, that the answer involves civil disobedience. For many rural and small urban churches, that will be the passive disobedience of staying hidden and keeping quiet. For many large urban churches, their civil disobedience is more active and militant. One unregistered pastor, Wang Yi, pastor of Early Rain Church in Chengdu, even advocates taking over the city one police station at a time.[13]

Registered pastors, on the whole, are a practical, realistic bunch. They are aware of their situation and realize that at any time it could deteriorate. In the meantime, they simply need to do what they can. One pastor reflected on this reality:

> Since the revolution, the Communist party has been in charge. The party ideology and the government ideology are Communist. That's the reality! But we give thanks to God that in this kind of society he is calling and gathering his people. There will necessarily be conflict. In this situation, the most important thing is prayer. God loves his people and will hear their prayers. In this society, temptation is very strong. There are temptations like power, money, and position, and many people dance to their tunes. This leads to many Christians' downfall. But if you don't give in and know you are a child of God, he will certainly lead you and see you through. With the government, you need to be able to distinguish what is important and what is not important. Faith must be held onto strongly. Administrative things we can compromise about and negotiate. We have had good relations with the government.

Framing the issue a different way, another pastor said, "The church is not free to protest in Tiananmen Square, but it is free to preach the gospel in church. Likewise, the government cannot preach atheism in church. We cannot go to the Great Hall of the People and say that atheism will certainly be destroyed. But we can preach in church that those who believe in Jesus will go to heaven and those who do not believe in Jesus will certainly go to hell." Echoing this sentiment, another pastor said that, "There's freedom to do anything on church property, but there are things you cannot do in public places." These comments reflect the government's unique interpretation of religious freedom: people are free to believe any way they want, but they can only express that belief on church property. This of course impacts most

---

13. For more information on Wang Yi and the Early Rain Church, see Li, *Religious Entrepreneurism in China's Urban House Churches*.

heavily on evangelism and social justice, things that are not allowed outside of church grounds.[14]

Registered church leaders tell me that they can compromise on nonessentials while holding firmly to the fundamentals of the faith. They believe that silence regarding political and social justice issues buys them the ability to continue preaching and teaching the basic Christian gospel. The things they are giving up allow them to hang on to what they most cherish. Up until Xi Jinping took power in 2012, both approaches, registered and unregistered, seemed efficacious, but now, all churches are watching and wondering about the future.

Paraphrasing another pastor, the church should be separate from the government. Scripture says we can honor the government and those in power, but we have no obligation to be involved in politics. If you are concerned about flags in church, your thinking is a bit narrow. If you go to a church in the US and see a national flag, you will not automatically conclude that there is no faith in that church, so why come to that conclusion about Chinese churches? Whether to have a flag or not is not an issue of fundamental belief. Actually, it is strange for Christians in China not to support the government. When Jesus came, he did not recruit people to rebel against the Roman government. In the face of the injustices of the Roman government, Jesus said that we are to love our enemy. Opposing the government is a matter of personal opinion, not a matter of faith.

Registered church pastors know how to survive, and they have a strong sense of priorities. One pastor said:

> The amount of religious freedom in the US is dangerous, while the situation in China is not bad. Christians do not need to be concerned about the government, but they need to worry about living in a way that honors God and helps spread the gospel. Some pastors are more concerned with the government than they should be. As a church, we are here to worship God, not to change the government. The government will always be here and we should just ignore it. Our focus should be on Christ's return rather than political ideology.

He added that, "Christians need to keep their priorities straight, focused on Christ and his return," an interesting statement from a pastor who supposedly cannot talk about the second coming.

---

14. Even though evangelism is not allowed off church property, at various times and in various places, I have been given tracts, invited to church, and have been told the gospel story.

Many pastors told me that the political and social activism of some unregistered church pastors is biblically unsupportable. Another pastor reflected about the unregistered Early Rain Church:

> Recently the government is taking a stronger line than before. Why is that? Has the government changed or has the relationship changed? You also have to contemplate whether the government's harshness is due to the government changing or due to your action. So, for example, the action and behavior of the Early Rain Church are quite extreme. When Jesus came, he was gentle and weak, so if people resort to violence they are likely not his followers. Christians should live out what they express in their beliefs.

Other pastors argued that it is simply not practical to oppose the government because the government controls everything. Even the large foreign companies need to obey the government's rules, one says, so how much more so the church, which has no standing in society.

THE FEARSOME SCENARIO

While trying to hold on to the relative peace of the last few decades, pastors do not deny that they sense more pressure and at least subtle opposition from the government. Xi Jinping and his Communist Party State have declared themselves all powerful in China, and they seem clearly to be advancing on that claim. The church, intentionally or not, consciously or not, realistically or not, is at least a roadblock, but maybe even a serious threat to the consolidation of power in the hands of Chairman Xi. The State does seem to be pushing at that roadblock. Some argue convincingly that the government's goal in recent actions is the complete subjugation of the church. The first step has been against the unregistered churches, seen in the closing of *Shouwang* Church and *Xian* Church in Beijing, *Ronggulii* Church in Guangzhou, and *Qiuyu* (Early Rain) Church in Chengdu. The unregistered church world has been served notice that vocal political action will not be tolerated. Possibly, the government is thinking that by silencing the four "troublemakers," the other unregistered churches will stay hidden and quiet.

The next step then would be against registered churches, and the new regulations of 2018 are undeniably aimed at them as much as they are against the unregistered churches. These actions include the newly enforced regulations about foreign involvement, the planting of Chinese flags and sometimes singing of the national anthem in church courtyards or sanctuaries, the shutting down of Sunday Schools, and the alleged corrupting of theology through Sinicization. The government could make life much more difficult for the registered churches. It could aggressively enforce all the new regulations, or it could actually push Sinicization to the point of outlawing the fundamental beliefs of Christianity.

To date, however, I have heard of no registered church pastors expecting the worst. They have been silent, maybe holding their breath, maybe hoping against what they fear, but mostly going on with their ministry as usual. The only changes, they say, have been the installation of national flags in church courtyards and finding ways to bypass Sunday school regulations, and these they can live with. They say that the government is simply flexing its muscles and reminding people who is in charge. They believe things will go back to normal soon. When I asked pastors about the VBS-type programs that I had led in the past, they acknowledged that these could not happen now, but, most added, "Just wait a couple of years."

A THIRD PARADIGM

In the arena of church-State relations, I have noted that Carsten Vala proposes two paradigms that are not mutually exclusive: domination-resistance and domination-negotiation. I would add a third paradigm that I experienced during my time in China: I call it the domination-circumvention paradigm. Like the other two paradigms, this approach acknowledges that the government holds all the power, that their hold is getting tighter, and that the government has been using its power indiscriminately. Many pastors affirmed this, recognizing that the church has no power and is helpless against the State. They added, however, that the church has something else in its toolbox, and that is its ability to maneuver. When I asked pastors and church leaders about government efforts to dominate their churches, almost all of them reverted, instinctively I think, to the supposition that they will surely find a way around whatever restrictions come their way. Everyone in China has grown up with the saying, *shang you zhengce, xia you duice,* loosely translated as "the government passes regulations, the people find a way around them," and registered church pastors are experts at this.[15] Anyone who has been in China for a while has experienced such things. In this new environment, Sunday School is called Nursery School, a summer Bible

15. For some creative examples, see Swells in the Middle Kingdom, "Churches, Posters, and State Propaganda."

Camp is called an English Camp, a sermon is called a lecture, and so on. I contend that this common, ingrained mindset of my Chinese brothers and sisters will always be their first response to whatever onerous regulations the government imposes.

Fenggang Yang provides an example of a way that registered church pastors pay lip service to the Party. They can often be heard mouthing the phrase, *aiguo, aijiao,* meaning love the country, love the church. Even though the word "country," or "Party," comes before the word "church," one pastor explained that the words are worth saying to gain legitimacy.[16]

A variation of this approach is that church leaders simply ignore what the government says or does. When I was preaching regularly at the English service of a Beijing church, government officials constantly visited the church, reminding the pastor in charge that this was not allowed. When the government official became adamant about my presence there, the church put a lay person in charge of the service, leaving the government officials confused because there was no one they could identify as responsible. It worked for five years!

The church/State relationship in China is fraught with tangible and intangible complications. Both bodies have fundamental ideological views regarding the role each should play in shaping Chinese society and government, and these views could hardly be more different. Put simply, the church believes that it should be able to function unhindered by the power or influence of the State, without the humiliation of registration. At the same time, the State claims the right to rule unhindered by any moral opposition from the church. Both claim to be seeking *hexie,* harmony. One thing seems certain; neither church nor State is going away or giving in.

16. Yang, *Religion in China,* 86.

4

A New Reality

Journal Entry, June 24, 2011, Hanzhong, Shaanxi Province

I left Guangyuan early in the afternoon and after a 4- or 5-hour bus ride I arrived in Hanzhong too late to do anything that day. Hanzhong is a typical medium-sized city with construction sites in every direction. Two KFC's and numerous coffee shops were within walking distance from my hotel.

The next morning, I set out to find the Hanzhong church. I passed the impressive St. Michaels Catholic Church and expected to see the Protestant church when I turned onto the aptly named "Friend Love Street." No church was in sight, however, so I asked several people for directions, and eventually found the Protestant church, set back from the street, almost hidden from view. No one was in the office, so I went into the sanctuary where one woman was praying on the kneeling benches and another was practicing the piano. I approached the woman practicing the piano and introduced myself.

She said that she was a *yigong*, or volunteer, and she explained that the pastors were not around, but she was willing to tell me what she could. The church could seat one thousand worshippers. Two pastors and eight evangelists served almost three thousand members. Although it is the only church in the city, there are many meeting points and five other churches within twenty kilometers or so outside the city, totaling about ten thousand believers in the area. The church offers a traditional morning and evening worship service on Sunday and two classes of Sunday school, along with many weekly meetings. The church also offers an early Sunday morning service, in which the scripture passages are first read by the leader and then repeated together by the people before being explained by the pastor or another leader. I was told this was a tradition dating back to the founding of the church when many of the people were illiterate.

As she talked, we were joined by one of the evangelists who told me that the church was founded in 1886 by missionaries of the China Inland Mission (CIM). Hudson Taylor himself, the founder of the CIM and one of the first Protestant missionaries in China, spent time there in the early days. She showed me a beautiful but crumbling house behind the church that had been used by the missionaries. Another missionary, Frank Moore, also spent time in Hanzhong, leaving just two years ago in 2009. I was told that members of his family still lived in Hanzhong, and that left me curious as to how he had managed to stay so long after the Communist takeover.

The church offers baptism once a year, typically baptizing about a hundred new Christians. The evangelist described the relationship with the government as "good; the government is supportive." When I asked about the strong points of the church, the evangelist responded just as so many other church leaders had. She said that the most wonderful thing about the church was the peoples' strong and pure love for the Lord. In contrast, the most serious challenge was the cults that lured members into strange thinking. Particularly mentioned were Eastern Lightning, a millenarian cult found all over China, and a new cult from Taiwan, introduced into China around 2017 and led by someone named Zuo Kun.

I had a 1:30 train to catch, so I declined their invitation to lunch and headed back to the train station. For four hours, my train followed a river valley through some of the most beautiful landscapes in China. Rolling hills, soaring mountains, and everywhere the shimmering green of rice paddies. As beautiful as it was, the farm homes looked tired and impoverished.

On the train, I passed the time chatting with a college girl from Hanzhong who was returning to school in Ankang. She would be graduating this year and was looking for a job teaching Chinese at the Jr. High or High School level. I was glad to accept her advice about hotels, because the one she suggested was excellent and cheap, and the KFC right next door satisfied my need for caffeine.

THE TEXT OF THE NEW REGULATIONS

There are regulations in plenty; no one will carry out the old ones. Nowadays everyone's drawing up regulations; it's easier writing than doing.

LEO TOLSTOY, *WAR AND PEACE*

While the actual text of the *New Religious Affairs Regulations* is, of course, in Chinese, the translated text, about twenty pages long, is available on the website *China Law Translate*.[1] Following is my review of the translated document along with my attempt to highlight the significant details of this new law.

The regulations are divided into nine chapters and seventy-seven articles. Starting out in a promising vein, Article 1 declares that the new regulations are in accordance with the constitution, and Article 2 follows with the guarantee that, "Citizens have the freedom of religious belief. No organization or individual may compel citizens to believe in, or not to believe in, any religion, nor may they discriminate against citizens who believe in any religion." While all this sounds promising, not mentioned is the fact that citizens may believe as they like, but they may not necessarily act on their beliefs. Nor is it mentioned that the government and the Communist Party are above the law.

Articles 3 and 4 have definitional problems. Article 3 is particularly important, stating that, "The management of religious affairs upholds the principles of protecting what is lawful, prohibiting what is unlawful, suppressing extremism, resisting infiltration, and fighting crime." The word *jiduan*, or extremism, is a code word for anything anti-government, and because unregistered churches are not registered with the government, they fall into the category of *jiduan*. *Sentou*, or infiltration, is another code word that refers to any sort of foreign involvement. Thus, right at the beginning, the enemies are identified. Article 4 is also foundational, laying out the State's role. "The State, in accordance with the law, protects normal religious activities, [and] actively guides religion to fit in with socialist society." Note that "normal religious activity" is purposely left undefined, thus guaranteeing that the government can apply it as broadly or as narrowly as it deems necessary. This article handily removes the guarantee of freedom of religion.

Article 5 reiterates the government's determination to outlaw foreign influence, stating that, "All religions shall adhere to the principle of independence and self-governance; religious groups, religious schools, and religious activity sites, and religious affairs are not to be controlled by foreign

1. See the Appendix for the English text of the new regulations.

forces." This provision makes it nearly impossible for foreigners to come in and help with ministry like the summer programs I ran from 2006–2015. Another concerning phrase is "religious activity sites." Basically, this refers to church buildings and possibly apartments used for gatherings of *jiuhuidian*, or registered meetings. This article is unnerving in its ambiguity.

Article 6 declares that all levels of the government should strengthen oversight of religion, while also strengthening the structures that deal with religion. The same article ensures that religious groups have the right to be heard by the appropriate governmental department.

Chapter 2 of the new regulations includes Articles 7–10 and deals with registering religious groups and with articulating the duties of religious groups and schools. This gets to the heart of the impasse between the government and the unregistered churches as one of the provisions states that religious groups must *xiezhu*, or aid, the government in implementing laws that preserve the religious rights of citizens. Ironically then, the church is expected to help the government take away people's religious rights.

Chapter 3 includes Articles 11–18, which focus on religious schools. Christian high schools or colleges are, and always have been, illegal in China, so the term "religious schools" refers only to seminaries and Bible schools. China has about twenty-five registered seminaries and Bible schools, with few if any new ones established in the last two decades. These new regulations will make it more difficult to start new schools. According to Article 12, religious schools can only be established by "duly registered churches or religious groups," which in this case would be local or provincial *Lianghui*. Article 13 states that the schools must register with the government, must submit training objectives and curriculum plans, must demonstrate a source of funding, and must get approval for appropriate sites and facilities. Article 17 states that schools can hire foreigners only with the consent of the religious affairs offices.

Chapter 4, one of the longest, contains Articles 19–35, and deals in detail with religious activity sites. As previously noted, "religious activity sites" is the coded phrase mostly for church buildings and occasionally for seminary or Bible school buildings. Article 21 states that the process for establishing a religious activities site is as follows: The group seeking to establish the site must get approval from the appropriate department and level of government. When construction is completed, the building needs to be inspected and approved. Then Article 22 states that when the construction has been approved, the site needs to be registered with the appropriate government department. Article 27 adds that religious activity sites will accept oversight and inspections by the religious affairs departments. This Article is worth quoting in full:

> Religious affairs departments shall conduct oversight and in-
> spections of religious activity site compliance with laws, regula-
> tions, and rules; the establishment and implementation of site
> management systems; the modification of registration matters;
> as well as religious activities and activities involving foreign en-
> tities. Religious activity sites shall accept oversight and inspec-
> tions from religious affairs departments.[2]

The article contains a warning about "foreign entities," stating that they, too, must accept oversight. Article 28 states that religious activities sites can sell religious books and goods, and that these church bookstores are now the only fully legal places to purchase Bibles. Article 32, interestingly, includes a provision that all levels of government need to include the establishment of religious activity sites in their urban/rural planning.

Chapter 5 includes Articles 36–39 and turns to "Religious Profession-als." Briefly, religious professionals must be affirmed by their religious group and they must report to the appropriate government oversight office. They also need to report when they leave a post. Finally, they are entitled to take part in social insurance.

Chapter 6 contains Articles 40–48 and is well summarized in Article 40, which reads:

> Collective religious activities of religious citizens shall, in gen-
> eral, be held at religious activity sites, be organized by religious
> activity sites, religious groups, or religious school organizations;
> and be presided over by religious professionals or other persons
> meeting the requirements of that religion's rules; and conducted
> according to religious doctrines and canons.[3]

Put simply, religious worship services or teaching may only be held in a lawful church and led by approved personnel. Articles 46–48 are concerned with publications in print or on the internet. Essentially, it states that any such publications must be approved by the government.

Chapter 7, Articles 49–60, deals with church finances and assets. Articles 49–50 state that all land and buildings used by the churches are protected. (Note, however, that in China, land cannot be owned; it all belongs to the state). All land and all buildings must be registered with the government. Article 52 declares that churches are nonprofit organizations. They can and should be engaged in charitable endeavors. Churches may receive

2. See Appendix.
3. See Appendix.

donations, but they may not exceed one hundred thousand RMB if from a foreign source without first being approved.

Probably the most crucial is Chapter 8, Articles 61–75, which takes up the subject of legalities and illegalities. Articles 61–62 promise government help if there is interference with religious groups or their meetings, either by government officials or by private citizens. Article 63 promises strict punishment for extremism (the vague term that is a code for cults and radical house churches). Article 64 delineates fines and punishments for anyone holding large scale religious activities without permission. Article 65 is a catch-all of illegal activities, in a sense reminding churches and schools of what they are not allowed to do. For example, schools may not violate requirements of their training objectives, churches may not accept foreign donations, and so on. The remainder of the chapter goes through all the topics of the previous chapters and lays out what sort of activity will result in what sort of punishment. Article 70 is particularly important because it involves dealing with foreigners or with foreign countries:

> Where, without authorization, religious citizens are organized to leave the mainland to participate in religious trainings, meetings, the hajj, or other such activities, or religious education and training is carried out without authorization, the religious affairs department, together with the relevant departments, is to order it to discontinue the activities.[4]

In other words, people may not organize trips overseas for education or training without permission. The concern here is that permission henceforth will be difficult at best to procure and at worst, impossible.

ENFORCEMENT

These religious regulations are not new. Although some wording has changed, most of the regulations were part of previous constitutions and were similarly articulated in Document 19, the comprehensive religious policy statement prior to this new one. With the ponderous title *The Basic Viewpoint and Policy on the Religious Question During Our Country's Socialist Period*, Document 19 was known for its attempt to preempt religious influence. Mickey Spiegel describes the government's determination "to harness the productive capacity of religious adherents in the interest of building a strong, modern state . . . without threatening the party's

4. See Apendix

primacy."[5] China has always had specific rules regarding religion, rules that if enforced, would make life very difficult for all types of Chinese churches. But most of the time, in most places, enforcement has been lax. There is still a good deal of laxity in enforcing rules, but change seems to be in the air. The question right now is whether the trajectory of tighter enforcement will continue, or if it will hold at its current level. In the West, we are conditioned to think that if there is a law, it will be enforced. But the reality in China has often been otherwise. C.K. Yang, in his writing about traditional China in general and the Qing Dynasty in particular, says, "Historical records show that, given *a critical situation,* many of the laws [regarding religion] would be enforced, whereas *in normal times,* they were tacitly ignored."[6] The key question is, "Are these critical times or normal times?" Judging by the escalating trade wars with the US, the full scale persecution, interment, and "re-education" of Chinese Muslim Uighurs in Xinjiang, growing tensions with Taiwan, and the charges and counter-charges arising out of the Coronavirus (COVID-19), it might well be the former.

The challenge has always been to figure out which laws the Chinese government will enforce, and then to what degree. When I was in China, for a number of years we arranged for several Chinese pastors and professors to attend a worship symposium in the US. This was counter to the spirit of Chinese law with its repeated warnings against foreign involvement, but we were able to do this many times, sometimes even including officers of the *Lianghui.* Several pastors have said that this would not work now. "We are in a critical time, not a normal time."

If the times are somewhere between normal and critical, then hopefully we have reached a resting place, a place where the government is willing to call a truce, so to speak. Clearly, Xi Jinping has sent a message with the stepped-up enforcement, a message reiterating that the government is in charge and churches need to exercise respect and restraint. For unregistered churches, the message was fortified by the closing of the four largest and most vocal unregistered churches in the country.[7] For the registered churches, the message was a gentler reminder through flags in courtyards and Sunday School closures. Maybe these have been reminders enough for moderation. As long as unregistered churches are not too vocal and not getting into politics, and as long as registered churches know their place, the government will not feel threatened and the status quo will be maintained.

5. Mickey Spiegel, "Control and Containment in the Reform Era," in *God and Caesar in China,* Kindopp, 40.

6. Yang, *Religion in Chinese Society,* 181.

7. The four churches are *Shouwang* and *Xi'an* churches in Beijing, *Rongguili* Church in Guangzhou, and Early Rain Church in Chengdu.

The worst fear is that times are closer to critical, and just as the Communist Party has initiated full scale persecution, interment, and "re-education" of their Muslim Uighurs in Xinjiang, so might they be determined to squelch the rising influence of Christianity. I find this scenario unlikely for a few reasons. While Islam is technically a recognized religion in China, this group is seen as having a separatist ideology and agenda that will not acquiesce to cooperation and ultimate subjugation to Xinjiang's Communist Party. Also, estimates of Uighurs in China range from one million to one million six hundred thousand people, and most of these people are concentrated in one area. In contrast, Christians are scattered all over China, and they number thirty million by conservative estimates and up to one hundred million by others. Furthermore, while the Muslim Uighurs share ideology with countries that China sees as threatening neighbors, Christianity is tied to many countries that China needs to deal with. While I see China as trying to limit the influence of Christianity amongst its citizenry, I do not see China as currently posturing itself to "take on" or shut itself off from relationships with the whole Western world.

REACTIONS TO THE NEW REGULATIONS

How then will the registered churches react? Most pastors seem to be accepting of the new status quo. The attitude of those I interviewed was mostly a tentative wait-and-see. They all acknowledged that things were tightening up and that ministry was more difficult, but their first response was that it might be temporary and that the best approach was to ignore things as much as possible. Correctly reading the actions and intentions of the government will be a major task for the church in the coming months and years.

As I write this, the new religious regulations have been in force for a little over a year, since the spring of 2018. Some pastors seem predictably adaptable in their reactions. "The church is still functioning normally" and, "ministries go on as usual," and, "up until now we have not noticed any effects." Many pastors mentioned that they have been ordered to fly national flags in their courtyards, and they comply without attaching much significance to it. One pastor calls it, "just a symbol of patriotism." (I might add, however, that he does not raise the flag unless a government official is coming to see it.) More seriously, pastors must deal with the outlawing of Sunday schools. Again, I've seen some clever circumvention techniques as pastors have simply changed the name of their Sunday school to a label that the government does not red-flag. Yesterday's Sunday schools have become today's "*tuoersuo*," or nursery schools.

Regarding flags and Sunday school, we must keep in mind the backstory. Neither of these issues came out of nowhere. National flags have always flown in the courtyards and offices of many Chinese churches, just as they do in many American churches. Likewise, Sunday school has always been illegal in the People's Republic of China, and churches have always found ways around this prohibition. Of course, we feel concern for our brothers and sisters in China, but rather than panicking, we may do well to adopt the attitude of most Chinese Christians with whom I've had contact: "We've dealt with such things before, and we'll figure out a way around them."

One of the new regulations requires that pastors take classes that explain religious regulations, taught by State Administration of Religious Affairs personnel. One pastor just shrugged and said that it's all part of improving rule by law. Another said that if the government wants to issue rules and regulations, there is not much you can do about it. This is just another indication that pastors generally try to avoid the government as much as possible. One Beijing pastor somewhat more hopefully concluded that "The government cannot dictate to churches what to believe or what to do. That would be illegal." He is hopeful that the constitution carries some weight.

Not surprisingly, still others felt that the new restrictions were positive and advantageous for the churches. One pastor offered this well-nuanced opinion:

> I have been studying the new regulations. On one level, the new policies indicate that the government recognizes the existence of the church. Since the new regulations give the church its own space in which to work, they give it legitimacy in society. From another perspective, the new regulations help to bring order to all religions. As long as the regulations do not conflict with religious beliefs, they are helpful. If they do conflict, then Christians need to ask God to move the government to change what is unjust. There's always been conflict between religion and the State. The Western and Eastern churches have different views. In the West, religion takes priority over the State, while in the East, the church has always been subject to the State. Throughout history, there have always been terrible governments. But no matter how bad the government, God is always present. If you are a Christian, no matter what the circumstances, you should always trust God, and no matter what the circumstances, you should always share the gospel. If there are minor differences, we can always negotiate with the government.

One pastor put it this way: "The government is creating a space that a registered church can operate within. There will be trouble only if a church goes outside that space." These pastors seem to be saying to the authorities, "If you allow us to operate unhindered in our own space, we will not try to move out of it."

But what exactly is that space? And who decides? Up until now, the space has been church grounds. Are these pastors speculating that their space could grow or change? Are the pastors thinking about more than just physical space? Or is it a matter of a sphere of influence or activity? The government may be telling the churches, "You may operate and maybe even grow within the religious sphere, but stay away from the social, the political, etc." Perhaps these pastors are describing a hoped-for, or ideal situation. At any rate, no one expects that the churches will be able to progress unhindered.

"Unhindered" would be a large step indeed. One pastor puts these aspirations within the context of Chinese history. Unlike in the West, Chinese government has never been hospitable towards religion, and to expect otherwise would be foolish, indeed. He fears that, more likely, intensified persecution lies on the horizon. As always, he concludes, Christians need to have great faith, and great perseverance, and do what God has always called them to do.

The effects of the new regulations will not be the same everywhere. The new regulations seem to be more onerous for rural areas. One church worker in a rural area said Sunday school has been completely shut down in her area and one of the churches in this area was forced to move Wednesday night worship to Sunday. An unregistered group in this area was closed down and many hundreds of books confiscated.

A major effect of the new regulations is a new system of church oversight called *yitang daidian,* which means "use the churches to supervise the meeting points." In China, the large churches are called *jiaotang.* Beijing has about twenty of these large churches, along with many smaller groups called *juhuidian,* or meeting points. The new legal structure puts the *juhuidian* under the authority of a large *jiaotang.* Actually, most of the meeting points have always been attached to one of the large churches, depending on them for personnel to preach and administer the sacraments, but it has always been an informal arrangement. Now the relationship is being formalized, with the large churches having a broader authority over the meeting points, and also a greater responsibility. One pastor in a semi-rural area described it this way:

The meeting points can be large or small, they may or may not have a pastor, and they may meet in homes or in rented places. But they need to recognize that they are under the authority of the large church. Also, groups like the local police and "peacekeepers" are expected to keep watch over the meeting points. They will ask questions like, "How many people attend?" "What are you doing?" "What sorts of people are attending? "Who is preaching or teaching?" The result is that things are now more restricted. Also, the "street patrol" will keep their eyes open for unregistered church meetings and report those to the police. Sometimes people need to show their ID when they enter the church and it is noted whether you are a local resident or a transient. This is only at the meeting points for now, not at the big church.

While this pastor recognizes that things are more restricted, she also notes the benefits for safety. Her church does do some reporting to the government about Christmas attendance, but once when the government wanted to register everyone present at a worship service, she refused.

INSIDERS AND OUTSIDERS

According to most pastors, the new regulations seem to have a particular focus. One pastor told me that after her conversation with the State Administration of Religious Affairs, she concluded that the unregistered churches were being targeted. She noted a particularly troublesome name change. The new official designation for registered churches is *tizhinei*, the Chinese term for "inside the system," while the new name for unregistered churches is *tizhiwai*, meaning "outside the system." These have replaced the words *dengji jiaohui* and *meidengji jiaohui* or "registered and unregistered." The names for these churches have thus gone from being based on something they do (register or do not register) to being based on something they are (insider or outsider).

Most likely, the new regulations are targeting the rise of heterodox sects. If so, then the government will be looking closely at the differences between these groups and the "legitimate" churches, and here a new problem begins. There is, of course, no clear formula for determining just what constitutes a heterodox sect, nor is there a specific guideline as to what distinguishes heterodox beliefs and practices from "orthodox" Christian beliefs and practices. That the State intends to make such determinations bodes poorly, I think, for many heterodox groups, while it also adds to the absurd, and I propose impossible, situation of an atheist government determining religious orthodoxy.[8]

FINDING A WAY AROUND

The Chinese have a saying, *Shang you zhengce, xia you duice,* or "The government issues policies; the people find a way around them." The Sunday school name change is a good example of this, as are the alternate locations and the new anonymous names for summer kids' programs. Likewise, foreigners can preach as long as no one calls it preaching and/or does not report it. One pastor said that reporting is too complicated anyway, so it is best to do what must be done, and just don't get around to reporting anything.

Never discount the ingenuity of Chinese citizens to live below the radar of their government. A great example of this is how to acquire Bibles in China. Since the promulgation of new religious policies in February of 2018, many new rumors have surfaced, the central one being that Bibles in China are no longer allowed to be sold anywhere but in registered church bookstores. First, a bit of background: Since the Communist takeover in 1949, it has always been illegal to buy and sell Bibles outside of the registered church bookstores. This had always been strictly enforced, but around 2008, Bibles began showing up in religious bookstores,[9] and by 2010, Bibles were appearing on the internet through online shopping sites like Taobao. Then in 2018, after Xi Jinping consolidated his power and promulgated the new religious policies, it once again became difficult to find Bibles for sale.

Not impossible, just more difficult. In 2019, a friend in Beijing introduced me to various ways to find and purchase Bibles online. In the coffee shop where we met, he showed me how to do an internet search, not for *shengjing,* which means Bible in Chinese, but rather for *heheben,* which is the Chinese name for the *Chinese Union Version.* Many people had told us that while we could order a Bible this way, we would never see it delivered, but that turned out to be untrue because we ordered a Bible right then and there, and it arrived at my friend's home the next day. Besides this site, anyone can access Bible study apps that often contain the whole Bible, and for those with the requisite language skills, English Bibles are still sold online. In addition to all of this, pastors and teachers regularly post sermons and

---

8. Indeed, it is difficult for any person or group to objectively define orthodoxy without being influenced by the group or person being evaluated.

9. The religious bookstores were allowed to sell religious paraphernalia and some religious books, but not Bibles.

biblical studies online. And of course, Bibles are readily available at registered church bookstores.

One of the pastors had a somewhat different take on how to deal with the new regulations. He warned the government about drawing the boundaries too narrowly, saying that would lead to more extremism. Then he had this to say to the church:

> If pastors and church leaders talk too much about the new regulations, the people will no longer come to church. The church has to talk about love, service, and care. These make up the unchanging heart of Christianity. We need to talk about how to spread the gospel. Really there are no changes brought about by the new regulations. Whether now, a half year from now, or a year from now, or until Jesus returns, we have to continue to talk about the good news of Jesus and of his love, service, and care. We need to do this even if the government makes changes. The government may change, but people still need Jesus. That doesn't change.

Virtually all of the pastors I know in China would say "Amen!" to this. The reality, however, is that continuing to talk about and serve Jesus is becoming more difficult by the day. The time may soon come when pastors, and all Christians, will have some difficult choices to make. I appreciate how another pastor reminds us to keep our eyes on God rather than on the government:

> Last year (2018) the government started promoting the *sijin,* or four advances: the Chinese flag, construction, the principles of socialism, and traditional Chinese culture. Now most churches have flags in the courtyard and propaganda posters on the outside walls. Most pastors do not see this as problematic. We don't need to make a big deal about it. If you overreact, you just draw the attention of the government. The flag is simply a sign of the country. We as Christians have a complete understanding of the meaning of life. We are sons and daughters of God. We do not belong to this world but to God. God has put us in this time and this place and we need to live a God honoring life in it. The question is: do we focus on Christ and what he calls us to or do we focus on the world? If our hearts belong to Jesus then we will live for him. We try to focus on training and on Jesus Christ. Even in this situation we can believe that God will see us through. And we try to promote the safety and growth of the meeting places. What we need to do is protect our churches and see that they grow.

5

The Debate over Sinicization

Journal Entry, June 27, Xiangyang, Hubei Province

Halfway through my month-plus journey from the south of China to the north visiting churches, I am getting disoriented. Days and cities flow into each other like branches of a river. It is getting difficult to keep track of what day it is and where I am, and today I woke up in a city with its own identity problem. Depending on who I ask and what sign I read, I am in either Xiangfan or Xiangyang. I noticed nothing particularly distinctive about this town. Like countless others, construction sites are hurling it into the modern world. I headed to Xiangyang Church early in the afternoon, making sure to wait until after the normal nap time of 1:00–2:30. At the church I found Pastor Zhu. She was one of three pastors at the church, all women. Pastor Zhu told me that the church was founded by Lutheran missionaries in 1891. Among them was a Canadian missionary whose Chinese name was Rang (or Rong) Fulin. There must have been quite a few missionaries since they started two schools and a hospital in addition to the church. The church was originally shaped like a cross and stood until 1997 when it was demolished to make way for the current large, mid-twentieth century American-style church building.

The church is led by the three pastors and two evangelists. The current building seats all of its one thousand five hundred members. The pastor estimated that there are about ten thousand believers in the area, worshipping in various meeting places, all overseen by the pastors or evangelists from this church. There is only one Sunday service, although a second service is being contemplated. Sunday School meets during the worship service, and a youth meeting and a service for the deaf and dumb convene after the main service. The church offers a leaders training meeting on Tuesdays, a singing and testimony meeting on Friday, and a service on Thursday to commemorate those who have died. (Sadly, this seems to be a weekly service.) There are two baptism services each year with one hundred or more baptized each time.

When I asked about the strong points of the church, Pastor Zhu said that it was a stable congregation and they were not dealing with unmanageable growth. While she considered the stability to be a good thing, she admitted that some people criticized the church for being too staid and not lively enough. Like so many others, Pastor Zhu identified cults as the major problem facing the church. Sometimes cult members came into the church building and tried to persuade members to leave with them, claiming that there was "no salvation in this church." She identified Seventh Day Adventists, Eastern Lightning, as well as some charismatic house churches as the main offenders. She did add, however, that not all house churches were like that. Also, like so many other pastors, she acknowledged the problem of meeting the pastoral needs of one thousand five hundred parishioners with such a small staff.

I left the church in time to catch a 3:10 bus to Nanyang, traveling today from Xiangyang in Hubei province, through a part of Hunan province, and ending up at Nanyang in Henan province. This bus ride was a miserable experience and so telling about the lack of infrastructure to handle the mad push to modernization happening all over China. When I boarded the rickety, old, dirty, fifteen-passenger bus, there were only eight passengers, so I had my own two-seat area. One bright spot. But then I saw that the bus was stopping every couple of blocks to pick up more riders, and shortly, the seat next to me was the last to be filled. (No one dares to sit next to a foreigner.) Meanwhile, behind me, a woman and her "little emperor" saw me as a foreigner to heckle. As the mother grinned, the child screamed at me, hurled English gibberish at me, and drooled on me while I did my best to feign sleep.

Although there was an expressway from Xiangyang to Nanyang, the driver took an old highway that meandered through semi-rural areas just busy enough to provide one traffic adventure after another. At one point, the bus came to a stand-still behind a long line of large dump trucks in the road ahead of us.

The road ahead seemed to be clear, and the delay puzzled me, but then I noticed that the bridge up ahead was closed to any vehicle bigger than a small car. After a long, hot, miserable hour, the bus started up again, and I saw that we were following the dump trucks off the main road and onto a dirt path clearly only wide enough to accommodate one vehicle. But sure enough, as we bumped along behind the dump trucks, semis, and an assortment of buses, we were passed by just as many going in the other direction. It took us a half hour or more to navigate less than a kilometer and reach the other side of the riverbed. From start to finish, I saw no police or traffic controllers in sight. Who was in charge? Why had all of those trucks avoided the main highway? The bridge had obviously been out for a long time. Why hadn't the bus company rerouted its driver?

SINICIZATION

Sinicization is the natural process by which non-Chinese societies, or in this case, religions, come under the influence of Chinese culture. Missionaries typically refer to this as contextualization, and everyone sees it as inevitable, predictable, and a good thing. The story of Christianity is actually the story of its spread to other countries, other cultures, changing and being changed by each. In China, however, Sinicization has become a broiling controversy because, ironically, the molding of Christianity into Chinese culture seems to be emerging, not in its normal progression, from a grassroots, gradual change, but rather from a top-down, government-launched initiative. Rather than Christianity gradually influencing and seeping into the hearts and minds of the people, the Chinese government has determined that it should take the initiative and assertively mold Christianity into its culture. Unusual at best and alarming at worst, as of 2015, all church leaders are required to attend classes on how to think about Christianity in Chinese socialist terms. Not surprisingly, many members of unregistered churches and many conservative Christians, typically from the US, argue that the government has launched this drive in order to mold Christianity in such a way that it is not only supportive of Chinese socialism, but, more seriously, that it is intended to change the very nature and heart of Christianity.

THE BACKGROUND—THEOLOGICAL
RECONSTRUCTION

The current push of the government to Sinicize Christian theology has a not-too-distant backstory, generally known as *shenxue sixiang jianshe*, or Theological Reconstruction or Theological Construction. It traces back to Bishop Ding Guangxun, also known as K.H. Ting,[1] who was influential in the Three-Self Patriotic Movement since the early years of the People's Republic. He had held various high offices in the church, including director of the national *Lianghui*, head of Nanjing Jinling Seminary, and various administrative posts in high-ranking government offices. Philip Wickeri, biographer of Ding Guangxun, starts his biography like this:

> In 1998, K.H. Ting persuaded the Protestant leadership in China to approve a resolution on strengthening "theological reconstruction" in the Chinese church. He argued that greater attention needed to be given to theology in order to facilitate the adaptation of Christianity to socialist society. Theological reconstruction provoked a wide-ranging debate on the future of Christianity in China, which continues to this day.[2]

As quickly as Ding's program of theological reconstruction was approved and adopted by the national *Lianghui*, opposition arose from both clergy and lay people across the country.[3] While Ding's new theology alarmed people on many fronts, the main concern was over Ding's weakening of the doctrine of justification by faith. In both unregistered and registered churches, Protestant leaders rejected theological reconstruction as a set of doctrines forced on them from above with a definite political agenda,[4] and they clearly would never acquiesce to an ideology that challenged their most precious and central doctrines of faith. In this and in other positions, he clearly undermined the fundamentalist and evangelical understanding of salvation by grace through faith.[5] Additionally, Ding's emphasis on "God is Love" to the exclusion of other divine characteristics discounted the doctrines of sin and judgment. The foundation of Christianity was no longer

---

1. For a biography of Ding, see Wickeri, *Reconstructing Christianity in China*.

2. Wickeri, *Reconstructing Christianity in China*, 1.

3. Wickeri, *Reconstructing Christianity in China*, 348. Vala, *The Politics of Protestant Churches*, 68.

4. Wickeri, *Reconstructing Christianity in China*, 352. Vala, *The Politics of Protestant Churches*, 74.

5. Wickeri, *Reconstructing Christianity in China*, 350. Vala, *The Politics of Protestant Churches*, 68.

one of personal repentance, forgiveness, and grace, but rather one of social responsibility and work ethic.[6] Ryan Dunch, Professor of Chinese History at the University of Alberta, wrote that Ding and his followers produced a theology that "was out of step with the faith held by most Chinese Protestants."[7] Carsten Vala sums up the failure of the initiative:

> Despite top level TSPM support for the campaign, Protestants reacted negatively at the grassroots across the country. Most pastors in official churches and many believers rejected the new ideas. According to one Hunan Provincial association official, 98% of the official churches rejected Ding's original formulation of Theological Reconstruction because it required changes to the doctrine of justification by faith.[8]

OPPOSITION TO SINICIZATION

Because of the widespread opposition, theological reconstruction never saw much traction, and left in its wake understandable suspicion of any government initiative to rework the Christian message in any way. Many Chinese pastors, and many more foreign Christians, committed to holding fast to the traditional Christian message and to resisting any attempts to change or mold it. One Chinese pastor referred to Sinicization as a political movement that fits into Xi Jinping's political ambition. He contends it is not like contextualization because its purpose is to reinterpret the Bible to fit into Xi's program.

In a surprising move, the *South China Morning Post*, on March 16, 2019, had this to say: "The push to 'Sinicize religion,' introduced by President Xi Jinping in 2015, is an attempt by the officially atheist party to bring religions under its absolute control and in line with Chinese culture."[9]

One does not have to look far to find alarmist claims in Western media, warning that the government's goal is to change the basic beliefs of Christianity through reeducation of pastors and retranslation of the Bible.[10] In this vein, one pastor fears that Sinicization is part of a broader political agenda. He sees it as a political tool that can be used by the government to ward

6. Wickeri, *Reconstructing Christianity in China*, 350.

7. Dunch, "Christianity and Adaptation to Socialism," 178.

8. Vala, *The Politics of Protestant Churches*, 89.

9. Gan, "Beijing Plans to Continue Tightening its Grip."

10. Besides *ChinaSource*, another publication that presents a more balanced view is *Christianity Today*.

off the encroachment of Western powers. Its purpose, he says, is connected with President Xi's plan to turn China into a world power, second only to the US. He wants to see Chinese people begin to be proud of their own culture. As part of this, he feels that all religions should disconnect from all foreign influence and religion should be subservient to the government.

Some pastors tell me that this talk about the government wanting to help the churches is utter nonsense. After all, what kind of Communist authoritarian state would be interested in helping Christianity in any way whatsoever? They contend that it is simply another case of the registered church falling into the trap of government propaganda.

SUPPORT FOR SINICIZATION

While Theological Reconstruction is the most recent attempt at Siniciza-tion, a more benign Sinicization can be traced back to the arrival of the Nestorians in the seventh century AD, and possibly several centuries earlier with the arrival of Buddhism in China. Nestorious's theology clearly bent itself to accommodate both Buddhist and Daoist mindsets,[11] and this has been continuing, intentionally or unintentionally, ever since. One pastor said:

> Sinicization is nothing new. Christianity has been Sinicizing ever since first coming to China. Foreigners even had to use the Chinese language, otherwise the Chinese wouldn't understand. Today, Sinicization has several meanings. One meaning is that the Chinese church needs to have its own Chinese testimony. These testimonies should connect with Chinese society. Also, Chinese have to have their own understanding of their faith. For example, Chinese society has been going through huge changes, especially in economic development, so now Chinese feel good to be Chinese. In that kind of society, how does the church testi-fy to the faith? If the church is left behind by social development, then it is without testimony. Also, we have to change people's thinking that Christianity is a foreign religion and Jesus Christ is a foreign God.

I appreciate the emphasis here on the Chinese having their own indig-enous testimony and understanding of the faith as well as their determina-tion to remain relevant. One pastor put it this way:

---

11. Bays, *A New History of Christianity in China*, 9–10.

The Sinicization of Christianity has been going on in China for a hundred years or more. Then it wasn't known as Sinicization, but as Contextualization. It is basically presenting the gospel in a way that is understandable and easy to accept for Chinese. We have to ask what is the heart of Christianity, and how do we bring that to our society?

Even though Sinicization is being thrust onto the church from the top-down, that is, from government initiative, many pastors see Sinicization as a complement to their efforts to teach their members that the church has a purpose and a role in society. One pastor noted that church leaders were awakened to the reality that the Chinese church needed a theology that fit the Chinese situation, perhaps the most visible being a stronger emphasis among registered church pastors and members on the importance of social involvement. For some pastors, the government initiative has given them permission for the first time to think and talk about these issues.

Another pastor shared his thoughts:

Sinicization doesn't just consist of surface changes such as the insertion of Chinese faces in paintings. Rather, it should be focused on helping the church find its proper place and role in today's society and helping the church influence society. The church should be more involved in social welfare, for example, helping the elderly, orphans, widows, etc., and to comfort those who are weak and lonely. Hopefully, Sinicization will encourage Christians to leave the church courtyard and go out to the society and spread the gospel. Jesus entered this world and carried the cross. Christians should do likewise. When ministering to the poor and the sick, we should not be preaching at them. We just love them.

The fact that this pastor thought Sinicization may encourage people to leave the church courtyard to evangelize is particularly striking. Remember that leaving church property to evangelize is strictly illegal, and yet this pastor and others are increasingly aware of the importance of getting the message of Christianity well planted into the evolving modern Chinese culture. If Sinicization results in a theology that resonates with the Chinese experience, then that theology will be easier to understand and accept. These ideas are most striking because they are a result of, or in spite of, pastors and church leaders having to sit through several weeks of government sponsored classes on this topic. Does the government even realize how empowering this initiative is for some Christians in China?

Carsten Vala offers yet another way to think about Sinicization. He writes about "the public transcript," or the public display of conformity to the official agenda.[12] Joann Pittman and Kerry Schottelkorb of *ChinaSource* explain this further in *Christianity Today*:

> Once an official agenda has been announced (in this case, Sinicization) all sectors within society must publicly display that they are "following the line," and their public transcripts must conform. This is helpful for us to understand the rhetorical context for the documents and remarks coming from Chinese Protestants.[13]

Exemplifying this, in April of 2018, the TSPM leader Xu Xiaohong announced that after much study, the TSPM was embarking on a five-year plan to deepen support for Sinicization. According to Xu, the aim is:

> To deepen the establishment of theological thought in the new era, promote the harmonious and healthy development of the church, exert a positive role for Christianity and practice the core values of socialism.[14]

Now Xu may be what Carsten Vala calls a "loyalist," that is someone in the Protestant establishment who actually supports such Party initiatives, or he may be simply conforming, saying what he needs to say in order to follow the established agenda and be able to continue his work in the church.

Another pastor, in a more hopeful and somewhat defiant tone, sees Sinicization as a powerful religious (rather than political) tool:

> This movement, the Sinicization of Christianity, is designed to make evangelization more effective by making Christianity more understandable from a Chinese perspective. Matteo Ricci[15] is an example. Even church architecture can be Sinicized. If the Sinicization of Christianity means what some foreigners have said—changing the basic beliefs of Christianity—that doesn't make sense. What would we preach? What would we teach? So when we come to church we simply need to preach Jesus crucified. How can we do other than preach repentance

12. This term is defined by Vala in *The Politics of Protestant Churches*, 11–15.

13. Schottelkorb, "China Tells Christianity to be More Chinese."

14 . Schottelkorb, "China Tells Christianity to be More Chinese."

15. Matteo Ricci was one of the first Jesuit, Roman Catholic missionaries in China. He spent several years in Macao before settling in Beijing in 1601. He is known for his attempt to blend into Chinese society. He wore Chinese clothes and lived in a Chinese manner. He became an expert in Chinese language and philosophy, even debating matters at court.

and new life in Jesus? If we don't do that, we may as well just be another social club.

I heard similar opinions expressed by many pastors, one who said that in promoting Sinicization, the government was trying "to help people" to understand Christianity from a Chinese perspective. A related goal was to point out similarities between traditional Chinese culture and Christianity. This pastor believed that this was God's good plan for the church. "Previously," she said, "Christian examples and theology were all Western. With this movement, Chinese can discover how God works within their culture and daily life." She repeatedly emphasized that in promoting the Sinicization of Christianity the government is certainly not trying to redefine the basic doctrines of Christianity. If that indeed happened, she too said the pastors would not know what to preach.

More pastors mentioned how Sinicization would help them to use every day Chinese examples and stories in their preaching, a new way to connect the gospel to everyday Chinese life. One said: "In my opinion, Sinicization has to do with better bringing together traditional Chinese culture and Biblical culture. For example, filial piety is emphasized in scripture and also in Chinese culture. Sinicization also encourages us to use everyday examples in our sermons. This makes faith much more personal. And it encourages people to use their own way of thinking to understand their faith."

Another pastor said that Sinicization has to do with "right living in family and society." He added that as Christians, we still look to the Bible as our guide for living.

Yet another saw it as part of church-State relations:

> Another goal of Sinicization is that religion develops along with and as part of society, rather than opposing the government's development. Should the church support the government? Yes! If the government is working on social development, the church should at least think about the problem of social development. In the past, when the church came to China, it was always involved in social issues such as education and medicine. The church has always had a positive role in society. What we have to ask is "What is Christianity?" and "How do we bring that to our society?"

Yet another plausible theory is that the government needs the cooperation of the Christian church. Could it be that instead of suppressing an enemy, the State is trying to shape an ally? As Vala noted, there seems to be more church-State negotiation than there is State pressure on the church.[16] After all, the registered church does not pose a significant threat to the government. For the most part, these churches have been quiet and compliant. In contrast, the cults certainly do pose a threat. Wouldn't it make sense to be able to distinguish clearly and easily between churches and cults? A key way of doing that would be to encourage registered church pastors and theologians to develop a theology that clearly distinguishes them from the cults. Sinicization could also set clear boundaries between the Chinese church and Western churches, thus accomplishing another goal of the government. Based on what has happened so far, it seems that Sinicization is leading more to negotiation and cooperation than to confrontation.

FUTURE DIRECTIONS

Most pastors seem to be approaching Sinicization with the predictable Chinese fortitude that I have come to respect. They work tirelessly for the Lord and live daily with the surety that the Holy Spirit is the strongest force in their lives, more powerful than any government could ever be. They give me hope. They are confident that the government will not succeed in changing the basic beliefs of Christianity. They say that if the government tried, pastors and church leaders would refuse to obey. Most also felt that Sunday schools will not be discontinued, if for no other reason than a practical one; because parents cannot leave their children home unattended, the church will always have to provide something. Pastors also affirmed their conviction that going along with Sinicization does not translate into support for the government, and the training seminars in Sinicization do not influence their belief or their faith. They also noted that if, as rumored, the government publishes its own translation of the Bible, they would never use such a thing.

So many pastors reiterated the positives of Sinicization. If Christianity becomes more understandable, more accessible to the average person, then evangelization will be easier. Many pastors intend now to use more Chinese examples and stories in their sermons. This was always an option, of course, but having a nudge has been helpful. And clearly, pastors anticipate an enhanced standing in society and a greater part in community programs. While this last hope seems dubious to me, pastors have a great interest in it. One pastor summed up what most said in one way or another: "If you are

16. Vala, *Politics of Protestant Churches*, 200.

deeply rooted in Christ, then whatever regulation the government comes out with, it will not affect you." A pastor in Beijing said it this way:

> Sinicization has no meaning of supporting the government. We are supposed to obey the government; that's the duty of Christians. We also have to pray for leaders. I don't know what "support the government" means in this context. We are called to be good citizens. As Christians, we have two different allegiances. First of all, we give allegiance to God, and then we give allegiance to the government. As Christians, we need to love our country; loving our country is simply one of the ways in which we love God.

6

The Great Divide

Journal Entry, June 12, 2011, Kunming, Yunnan Province

Today, I called on Prof. Xing at Yunnan University. She was baptized and learned the basics of Christianity in the registered Trinity Church in Kunming. She later spent a year studying at Calvin College in Grand Rapids, Michigan. While there, she and Susan Felch from Calvin College cowrote a book that uses Bible stories to teach English to Chinese students, and when she returned to China, she took a position teaching English classes at Yunnan University. She currently mentors more than two hundred graduate students. Soon after she returned to China, she switched her church membership to a house church. This piqued my interest, so I invited her out for coffee to hear more. She explained that she had been influenced by a number of Chinese Christians in the States, who had explained to her some of the differences between the registered and unregistered churches. She had been told that the registered churches do not have any systematic theological preaching or teaching, that the registered church receives significant influence, if not control, from the government, that many of the pastors are in it just for the salary, and also that in some places the registered church makes life difficult for house churches.

I explained to Professor Xing that the government has applied certain pressure and has certain rules for the churches; however, in my experience, these rules had in no way hindered churches from carrying out the fundamental activities common to any church. Given pastors' salaries, the allegation that they are in it for the money would be just laughable if it were not so cruel.

Professor Xing did add that things were different all over, and that in Kunming the relationship between the registered church and the house churches was quite good. She estimated that Kunming has more than one thousand house churches compared to the five registered churches. I was surprised to hear that her church was a "Reformed Baptist" church and was founded about fifteen years ago by a missionary from Kalamazoo, Michigan.

HISTORICAL OVERVIEW

Acrimony between registered and unregistered churches goes back to the early days of the People's Republic in the 1950s. Soon after uniting China, the Communist government set up the Religious Affairs Bureau, the government agency tasked with regulating the practice of the five legal religions: Buddhism, Daoism, Islam, Catholicism, and Protestantism. They also established "Patriotic Associations," one supervisory agency for each religion. The Protestant agency was named the Three-Self Patriotic Movement (TSPM). To be considered legal, a church had to register with this agency. Suddenly, all churches and pastors were forced to choose whether to cooperate and register with the TSPM or to refuse to register and go underground. A church either registered and became a legal church, or they did not register and became an illegal church. No middle ground was possible, and thus the great divide began. Many dissenting pastors charged cooperators with selling out to the government, and some TSPM pastors turned in their dissenting brothers and sisters who were arrested and, at times, put to death.

The religious situation worsened immeasurably in the mid-1960s with the onset of the Cultural Revolution. Religion was outlawed, the few churches still open were shuttered, and Red Guards were given free rein to attack believers at will. For more than a decade, many Christians, both pastors and lay people, were sent to forced labor camps. Thousands lost their lives. Some survived by becoming informants.

After the Cultural Revolution, the Religious Affairs Bureau and the Three-Self Patriotic Movement were reestablished, and the reopened churches were once again forced to choose whether or not to register with the government. Thus, the gulf widened. Those who were released from prison gravitated toward unregistered churches, while most of those who had not been in prison stayed with the registered churches.

Since 2000, the bitterness and division has lessened somewhat, although flareups continue. In 2010, for example, when many unregistered church leaders were planning to attend the largest gathering of the Global Missions movement, the Lausanne Conference in Cape Town, South Africa, the government denied their involvement and allowed only registered church leaders to attend. One unregistered church, the Early Rain Church in Chengdu, capital of Sichuan Province, then published in their bulletin, "Through this incident God has made visible the spiritual warfare between house churches and Three-Self churches."[1]

This pronouncement of spiritual warfare represents a new and disconcerting level of conflict, not only between unregistered and registered churches, but also amongst various types of unregistered churches. Now unregistered churches are taking sides over the issue of how political and anti-government a church should be. Generally, and predictably, while most rural churches are opposed to politicization, the urban churches generally take part in increased political action.

THE CONTOURS OF THE CONFLICT

Westerners continue to misread and misrepresent the relationship between registered and unregistered churches. Gerda Wielander describes it as follows:

> As far as Christianity is concerned, until recently—and certainly in the West—the entrenched paradigm was that Christianity was considered a foreign religion which was tightly controlled by the government; that the majority of Christians worshiped in "house churches" which uniformly stood in opposition to the official churches and the government; and that Christians were persecuted by an atheistic party.[2]

Nathan Faires describes the situation similarly, but points out that Chinese Christians do not see it in the same way:

> Foreign Christians talking about China tend to divide the Chinese church neatly into "official" and "underground," by which

---

1. Early Rain Church Bulletin, October 24, 2010. Thanks to Mary Ma for this citation.

2. Wielander, *Christian Values in Communist China*, 2.

they often connote a value-laden difference between the two groups in their freedom to be faithful to Christian orthodoxy: the official church is compromised by its relationship to the Chinese government, and the underground church is persecuted by a repressive regime for being a counter cultural prophetic voice. Chinese Christians do not necessarily engage in this same sort of conversation or find this bipartite analysis fruitful. This binary summary of the complex case is more a part of the foreign Christian perspective, less a part of the domestic.[3]

While it is convenient to accuse foreigners of misunderstanding and exaggerating the tension between the two types of churches, as Wielander points out, these Westerners ultimately get their information about the Chinese church from Chinese believers. There is undeniably a divide between the two types of churches, but Wielander argues that the reasons for the divide are more nuanced and complex than most Westerners realize.

The common terminological dichotomy of "official churches" and "house churches" implies clearly drawn lines between the two, when in reality the sector is diverse and varied. There are many reasons why people worship in one or the other type church; often the reasons are practical rather than theological, let alone political.[4]

Both scholars noted the popular, but not always accurate, view that Christians in China are suffering from intense State-initiated persecution, mostly directed at members of house churches. In reality, however, for the last decade or two, physical persecution or imprisonment has been rare. Instead, church buildings have been the target of persistent harassment. It has been much too common all over China for churches to be boarded up or even bulldozed, crosses removed, and goodwill efforts like Christmas programs and disaster response have been shut down.

Wielander and Faries also note that most foreigners are sure that the registered churches are, at worst, controlled by, or, at best, compromised by the government. In reality however, the everyday interaction between church and State is more negotiation and working together rather than churches being forced and coerced. Both government and church leaders may at times spout government rhetoric, but their actions often say something else.

It is worth repeating that when I asked pastors about challenges to the church, relations with the unregistered churches did not crack the top five.

3. Faries, The "Inscrutably Chinese" Church, 4.

4. Wielander, Christian Values in Communist China, 16.

This may be because it is just like the air: since it is everywhere, we tend not to notice it. Or it may be that the topic is too painful. Whatever the case, when asked directly about this topic, the pastors opened up considerably, and the answers were not consistent. One surprisingly common response was along the lines of, "We have no contact with unregistered churches," or "minimal contact." Some, while professing no contact, did know of some ministries that were jointly led by both registered and unregistered churches, such as services for people with handicaps. Some registered pastors have tried to reach out to unregistered churches, but with little success. One pastor even claimed that registered church personnel did not even know unregistered church basics like location, worship times, and programs. She also asserted that the registered churches have no way of knowing anything about "what is happening between house churches and the government."

The actual relationship between the two types of churches is much more diverse and complicated, although undeniably fractured and discouraging. Poor or no communication between the two groups is common and too often, talk about the "other side" reeks of bitterness, gossip, and exaggeration. Chen Jing acknowledges this, and faults, ironically, not the church members, but rather the government:

> Generally speaking, even with some goodwill gestures, communication, and cooperation at the grassroots level, there is deep-rooted distrust, tension, and even the occasional skirmish between them. The reasons behind this troublesome relationship are multi-faceted and complex. Among all the historical, theological, and cultural factors, the church-State relationship stands out as arguably the most decisive and critical factor behind this TSPM vs. house church split. You have an all-powerful communist party and a state that is determined to keep religions under its control.[5]

While Chen's analysis may be extreme, we cannot deny that the government does play its role, a role not so much directly supporting one team or another, but rather keeping the two sides suspicious and divided.

THE PASTORS SPEAK UP

Pastors of the unregistered churches regularly accuse the registered churches of preaching a liberal theology, of compromising with the government, refusing to aid unregistered churches, and of refusing to repent for betraying

5. Jing, "Reconciliation is Good, But . . . "

Christians in hiding during the Cultural Revolution. Vala also records instances of this charge:

> Some unregistered church leaders from the early 2000s to the end of the decade further claimed that official church pastors failed to preach the true Gospel message, implying that few worshipers in official churches will go to heaven. Such unregistered leaders called official churches *jiade*, or false, for adhering to state policies that they viewed as conflicting with biblical teachings.[6]

Carsten Vala gives another similar catalog of unregistered church criticisms of registered churches:

> Whether due to suspicions about doctrinal distortions, associational control, a lack of congregational autonomy, or neglect of missions work, many unregistered church leaders have considered official churches to be illegitimate for obeying the Party-state rather than God. Summarizing this view, an unregistered church leader flatly declared that the Three Self churches are not real churches because they have to follow the government, like every other [public] social organization.[7]

These are serious charges. The most disheartening truth about these negative views and attitudes is that they seem to begin with the church pastors and other leaders. Even the majority of unregistered seminary students I have talked with hold and propagate these strident and narrow views.

Similarly, registered church leaders and pastors complain about unregistered church leaders, accusing them of propagating false stories about the registered churches. Another all-too-common accusation is that registered church pastors preach a watered-down theology. One pastor talked about the issue of salvation:

> The fact that many house church members say there is no salvation in the registered churches is simply wrong theologically. One's salvation is up to Jesus, not which church you attend. Someone who says that there is no salvation in the registered church has a problem, because salvation is from God.

Yet another pastor talked about faith: "People in the house churches did not talk about faith, they only focused on their persecution. And they accused those who were not persecuted of having no faith."

---

6. Vala, *Politics of Protestant Churches*, 89–90.

7. Vala, *Politics of Protestant Churches*, 93.

Many pastors simply told me that they know nothing about their un-registered church brothers and sisters. One specifically said that because the unregistered churches do not share what is happening between them and the government, they do not know how to help them, and all they could do is pray. Another pastor echoed this and made several other points:

> Some house church leaders ask the registered church leaders if they are cooperating with the government. Also, they have asked, "Why don't the registered churches help us?" One reason is that we do not understand what is going on in the house churches. Also, we do pray for them and trust that God will lead. For a while the government allowed house churches to function. But as they got bigger, it became hard to know what was going on in them, and so the government clamped down. Also, we need to watch out for our own safety. We need to do what God has called us to do and not any more. We also need to contemplate what God is doing. Pastors especially need to think over what is from God and what is from the government. The bottom line is that we do not have the ability to do anything about the situation. But God does.

The registered churches continue to resent the unregistered churches for their unwillingness to register, for what they see as unregistered church's constant efforts to pull members away from registered churches, and for their determination to accuse the registered churches of being politically motivated.

Consistently, the concern about unregistered church behavior is linked to the concern about cults and the frequent tendency of both cults and unregistered churches to proselytize those in the registered church. One pastor said, "We are glad to discuss Christianity with them and are glad to welcome them to our church, but if they try to take our members away, then we will not allow them to participate." He added that while there are many good unregistered churches in Beijing, there are also many that are chaotic and cultish.

Another pastor had sharp criticisms: "Some house church leaders are not willing to be registered because they will lose their power and position. Often these leaders preach and teach against the registered churches. Some of the house churches do not care whether someone understands Christianity, they just want to baptize you. Some house churches can become cults and lead people away."

Closely related to the "unregistered church as cultish" charge is that "unregistered churches are *luan*," or unruly. Several pastors and lay people feel that the unregistered churches are too chaotic and their leadership structure is not orderly. I was told several times not to go to Henan province for this reason. One pastor gave this a racial or ethnic flavor: "Chinese need to be overseen. If they are not, they just do what they like. A lot of the house churches are that way. If there is no oversight, they just do what they want. Freedom becomes self-indulgence. And self-indulgence can lead to extremism."

Another pastor said this about Xi'an Church in Beijing and Early Rain Church in Chengdu, both recently closed by the government: "In regard to those two churches, if the government issues a rule, should Christians obey or disobey? These two churches are a bit extreme in their behavior and speech. So they set themselves up as an opponent. The government's goal through all this is to maintain stability in society."

As with most interpersonal problems, money is a point of contention between the churches. A number of registered pastors told me that some of the unregistered church pastors or other leaders are just "out for money." They are strictly opposed to registering, not because of doctrinal reasons, but because registering would make it easier for the government to investigate their financial dealings. The two main issues connected to money are how it is acquired and how it is used. The money allegedly coming into unregistered churches is not only from local contributors, but also from overseas, mainly the US. While I do not have any direct evidence of this practice, I have heard many people, Chinese and foreign, unregistered and registered, talk about it as common practice. The temptation, of course, is for the pastor who receives the money to keep it for personal use, and stories of extravagance are commonplace. There allegedly are pastors who own multiple expensive houses and cars, or who have an extensive collection of designer clothes. It should be pointed out that this kind of behavior is more common among cults than among unregistered churches, and most unregistered church pastors are dirt poor. It should be added that charges of "just being in it for the money" are also levied against registered church pastors.

POSITIVE SIGNS

While the situation may seem hopeless, there are positive signs. Many pastors and churches work cooperatively. One church or the other might sponsor joint training sessions. My wife attended a Sunday school teacher's training that was organized by an unregistered church but attended mostly by registered church members. Many young people church-shop both registered and unregistered churches. One unregistered church member told me that when their church was in need of someone to preach, the local registered church sent someone over. A pastor told me that an unregistered church pastor gave him a car when he needed one. Sometimes believers from unregistered churches that have no pastors go to a registered church to take communion. The list could go on.

One of the pastors concluded that it was time for both sides to sit down and talk. Many pastors mentioned that they had numerous friends who were from the unregistered church, and that they help each other out whenever possible. One specifically noted that there have been times when unregistered church members came to his church and afterward told him that it was totally different from their expectations. One pastor said simply that if unregistered church members have faith in Jesus, then, "We love and accept them as brothers and sisters in Christ." Another pastor, assessing the situation, took a subtle swipe at the government, saying, "In Christ's church, there is no insider or outsider." Vala points out some other positive signs:

> [Unregistered] Protestant congregations form by splitting off from TSPM churches and unregistered leaders also get trained in TSPM/CC seminaries, making the distinctions between unregistered and official congregations less stark than unregistered leaders' criticisms suggest. . . . Despite the variety of critiques launched against TSPM pastors, individual unregistered church leaders do seek cooperation with particular TSPM counterparts that they have come to trust. In short, unregistered groups spread through the help of pastors in official churches, despite the Party-state's agenda to draw clear organizational distinctions through registration processes and by granting institutional status to official congregations under TSPM/CC authority.[8]

Finally, a Beijing pastor left me with this thoughtful and realistic analysis:

> Most of the registered church pastors I know are fair and openminded. Whether one registers is not the most important thing. What's important is preaching the gospel and honoring and lifting high the name of Jesus Christ. The question to ask is whether your faith is pure or whether you are using it to make money. Some house churches have a negative attitude toward registered churches. We realize that maybe there are some misunderstandings or maybe insufficient information or maybe they are just listening to other people. I have had contact with some house

---

8. Vala, *The Politics of Protestant Churches,* 96.

church members and they say, "you don't believe such and such and your church doesn't teach the true gospel." So I ask, "Have you been there?" And they say "No." So I ask, "How do you know that we don't teach the pure gospel?" And they said they heard someone else say it.

The divide between registered and unregistered churches is not going away anytime soon. True, there has been progress, but it is local and patchwork. As long as unregistered church leaders continue to proclaim that there is no salvation in registered churches, reconciliation will sputter, and as long as registered church leaders refer to unregistered churches as cults whose pastors are only interested in money, there will be no cooperation. It is possible that changes in government religious policy will work to bring the different churches together. We have seen signs of this. Interestingly, when the government shuttered all churches because of the Corona virus in 2020, both registered churches and unregistered churches were forced to develop their online presence, and, sure enough, their messages are much more similar than they are different.

7

Strengths and Weaknesses

Journal Entry, June 30, 2011 Kaifeng, Henan Province

"Have Yourself a Merry Little Christmas." I have been continuously serenaded by this song since arriving at the hotel in Zhengzhou, Henan Province. It greets me when I wake up in the morning, accompanies my writing, and lulls me to sleep at night. It is coming from the stereo in a store near my hotel. I haven't discovered why they play that one song over and over and over again. It is disconcerting. Maybe it serves as a reminder that the real reason for Christmas, here as well as in the States, is consumerism. And of course, June is as good a time as any to buy stuff. At any rate, I will never be able to think of Zhengzhou without feeling like Christmas.

But now I am headed to Kaifeng, The Northern Song, the ancient capital of the dynasty that was the focus of my graduate studies years ago. I just couldn't miss the opportunity to stroll the streets walked by Su Dongpo, Wang Anshi, and Sima Guang, the scholars who occupied significant places in Chinese philosophy, literature, and politics. It was a bad decision. I emerged from the airconditioned bus into a boiling cauldron. Even Beijing's hottest, most humid days were no match for this. What had possessed Zhao Kuangyin, the founder of the Song Dynasty (960–1279), to choose such a place for a capital? I walked for as long as I could stand it, imagining Su Dongpo writing poetry at one of the tea shops, and then flagged down a *sanlunche,* a three wheeled vehicle, to take me to a church. Perusing the list of churches, the driver identified the West Gate Church as being the closest.

The West Gate Church, appropriately, is not far from the ancient west gate of the city. It is located along a river in an area that is being developed as a tourist attraction where many new buildings, built in the Song Dynasty style, are under construction. The church plans to get in on the action by building a traditional hallway and courtyard leading into its sanctuary. Tourist Evangelism. I was greeted by a woman who arrived at the church just after me. She was there to *zhiban*, to keep the church open and watch out for any visitors like me. She explained that she had spent five years working in New York but had failed to learn English. She became a Christian in New York, however, and decided to come back to her hometown to serve the church. Over my protests, she said she would call the pastor to see if he could come to talk with me.

I must have been quite a sight. Sweat was oozing out of every pore in my body. After about fifteen minutes, maybe sensing my discomfort, the woman ushered me into the pastor's office, which thankfully, had a large ceiling fan. In this office, I was able to more or less dry out by the time a young man, who I assumed was the pastor, came in and greeted me. He wasn't the pastor, but he was an evangelist who served at that church. He had graduated from Nanjing Seminary two years earlier, and was doing his compulsory three years of service before he could be ordained as a pastor. Li was a delightful young man, with a smile that lit up his whole face. He said he loved his work, especially preaching, and was looking forward to many years of being a pastor. But the pressing problem of this church was that there were not enough like him. Most of the current leadership was nearing retirement age, and there were not enough younger leaders to replace them. Sixty percent of the members are sixty and older, 30 percent are between thirty and fifty-nine, leaving only 10 percent below thirty years of age. There are one thousand two hundred members in this church, making it one of the largest of six churches in the city. Growth is not happening as quickly in this church as in some other areas of China. Baptism is held once every two years, with about one hundred fifty being baptized. The church is packed full for the morning service, but only the smaller sanctuary is used for the afternoon service. The worship order is traditional, but a unique factor is that they have two worship bands/orchestras. One of these is "Western," with guitars and drums; the other uses traditional instruments to play Chinese folk music. It seems each of these is involved in some way in worship once a month. The church has all the usual programs, plus a testimony meeting and a class to teach reading.

Mr. Li didn't tell me a whole lot about the history of the church. He did say that it was founded by *Xinyihui,* or Lutheran, missionaries in 1935 and the current building was built in 1997. After a bit more chatting, Mr. Li gave me a ride back to the bus station on his motorcycle. I purchased my ticket, got in line, and after a short wait, boarded the bus. The bus was so hot that even the Chinese were complaining. One young man tried to start the bus in order to turn on the air conditioning, but only succeeded in closing the door, making the situation even worse. I was sitting in a pool of my own sweat. Fortunately, this situation only lasted about ten minutes, after which we were off, air conditioner blasting. Two hours later, back at the hotel, I collapsed on the bed. "Have yourself a merry little Christmas!"

A NEW ERA

In 2019, I revisited West Gate Church in Kaifeng, and I found that life and ministry was going on pretty much as usual and no major changes had taken place. With the exception of Sunday school, all the regular worship services and programs continued. The government was enforcing the rule that children under eighteen could not enter church property, and this, of course, created logistical problems for the church. However, in good Chinese fashion where the government makes laws and the people find a way around them, the church had rented a space across the street and held Sunday school there. On a positive note, the demographics at the church had improved, with a more even distribution of all age groups.

Nowadays, not all churches enjoy the same freedoms that this one did. "Life and ministry goes on normally," is a statement that applied to fewer and fewer churches in 2019. It does still apply, for the most part, for churches in Beijing and a number of other large cities, but other churches are seeing more and more restrictions. I saw an example of this in the fall of 2019 at a church in Anyang in Henan province. This large church with several thousand attendees was founded in the 1880s by John Goforth, a Canadian Presbyterian missionary. The church has four pastors and a number of elders, who perform many of the duties of pastors. Not all is well, however. The local government had taken a number of actions. It had shut down the Sunday school. The church responded to this by organizing a class for mothers, who study the Sunday school lesson, which they then teach to their children at home. The government has also torn down three crosses from the church and ordered the church to fly the flag. In addition, the church has had to post pro-government posters on the church walls. The pastor was visibly angered as he explained all this to me.

Nearly everyone agrees that the registered church in China has entered a new and difficult era. The government is more and more insistent on claiming complete control over all aspects of society, and this includes the church. Under these circumstances how does the registered church go forward? What are the strengths and weaknesses of the church that impact on its struggle to stay viable in the face of growing government meddling? In answering questions like these, the pastors' responses were almost all ecclesiological and theological rather than political. Indeed, there is a strong aversion to becoming entangled with politics. Many told me that the reason for the downfall of Shouwang, Xi'an, and Early Rain churches was that they were too political. The question is whether the churches can survive without becoming overly involved with politics.

GOING FORWARD—WEAKNESSES

Most of the challenges to the church have been mentioned in chapter 2. Here I would like to focus on the churches' ability or inability to face and overcome these challenges. In other words, what internal strengths can the churches bring to bear on the challenges they face, and conversely, which challenges does the church face from a position of weakness.

An important weakness may be the inability of the church to meet the changing needs of Christians. A young congregation member at a large Beijing church described it this way: "In the last ten years the churches have been stagnant. They have not provided believers with more in-depth training in spiritual growth and discipleship. Because of that, the number of house churches in Beijing is increasing, and the number of people in the registered church is decreasing."

Actually, the registered church population is not decreasing, just growing more slowly, but her point is well taken. The typical urban Christian is more highly educated and more socially savvy. They are searching for answers to life's difficult questions and are looking to the church to provide these. They are longing for role models and mentors and spiritual depth. They are no longer satisfied with entry-level sermons that do not touch on their social and emotional needs. Neither can they identify with repetitive worship and music that is often straight out of the nineteenth century.

Without seriously addressing these needs, the church may continue to stagnate. Add to this a serious shortage of seminary students, as young people no longer find church work compelling.

Another weakness of the registered churches is a lack of community. A Beijing pastor described it this way: "The purpose of churches is to worship together and to be in community together. But being 'in community' is a big challenge for registered churches. There are too many people. Some churches have five thousand or more members. We are all brothers and sisters in Christ but we don't know each other. After the church service we need to leave because people are arriving for the next service."

He concludes by saying that some registered churches are starting small groups. Some churches are making this work, but their number is small. One example is the church in Anyang that I mentioned above. Corporate worship is held on Sunday morning. Then on Sunday evening, people come to the church for small groups. However, often the small groups become simply a Bible study dominated by a single leader. While Bible studies are also needed, they are not all that is needed. There is a deep need for sharing life and faith together, for being a community. There is a need to know and be known. But there is very little history of this sort of small group ministry in the registered churches. Leadership is hard to find, and even then, most churches simply do not have enough space to support a small group ministry. This is an area in which the registered church could learn from the unregistered church. Many of the urban house churches have been experimenting with small groups for several years now. Some of them may be willing to share materials and expertise.

And of course, community is not necessarily achieved solely through a small group program. It is a matter of investing in people's lives, rejoicing together and mourning together. Actually, it is closely tied to the other area of concern: discipleship. Any worthwhile discipleship takes a deep, long-term commitment. All of this runs into the busyness of life in big-city China. Often, people need to stay late at work or have jobs that take them out of town for several days or weeks. Having led small groups myself in Beijing, I know how frustrating scheduling can be. In the face of such difficulties, most pastors do not have the time, not to mention ability, to lay the foundations for such a program, and most parishioners do not have the training or experience to do so either.

The lack of pastoral care is also a weakness of the registered churches, as noted in chapter 2. One church member in Beijing noted that even when pastoral care is attempted, pastors tend to give general answers to specific problems. Pastoral caregivers are simply not familiar with and/or are not trained to counsel about many of the issues of contemporary life. For example, it is not acknowledged or recognized that the grief and depression resulting from losing one's partner is different from that suffered on account of losing a job. There are many of these issues, such as how to handle the specific difficulties of being a Christian in the workplace, or what to do if the person you want to marry is not a Christian, or how to honor parents and ancestors as a Christian, and the list could go on. Often these issues, and how to counsel these people, are not understood by the pastoral caregiver.

Over the last ten years (2011–20), these issues have gotten more serious due to the rise in consumerism. As an example, if a young man wants to get married, he must often have a good job, a luxurious apartment, and an expensive car. This has gotten to be more difficult with China's slowing economy, and now with the economic disaster brought on by the COVID-19 pandemic, the need for serious pastoral counseling continues to grow.

Yet another weakness is the lack of companionship and cooperation between church pastors. While it seems that the pastors within a given area all know each other, they do not seem to promote any deep connections. This also contributes to the lack of documents outlining the church's theology and ecclesiology. In fact, the lack of a defined ecclesiology may be a result of pastors lacking opportunities to meet and pray and study together.

Finally, some pastors weaken the church simply by their own immorality. The number of pastors, both registered and not, who have had to leave the church on account of marital infidelity or affairs of one kind or another is large and getting larger. In the decade or so that we attended a particular church, two pastors had to leave the church for this reason. The weakness is compounded because these situations are not dealt with openly.

GOING FORWARD—STRENGTHS

The strengths of the church are numerous. Surprisingly, given the shortage of leadership, especially pastors, one pastor said that the large and increasing number of Christians is a mark of strength. He reasoned that the more Christians there are, the more people will be reached with the gospel. Notice he did not say that the goal was more power or influence, which might be a typical Western goal. He said that more numbers simply mean that there will be more Christians. He is more concerned with the advancement of the gospel than the acquisition of political power or social standing.

This emphasis on evangelism is itself one of the prominent strengths of the church. In all my interviews with pastors, when I asked about the strengths of the church, the emphasis on evangelism was always at or near the top. And when I talk with lay people about their faith, they always bring up evangelism. This was true a decade ago when I made my trip to visit churches in 2011, and now it is even more so. While I used to see the older people sharing their faith, now I see that the younger people are becoming vocal too, and when these twenty–forty year-olds share their faith, it is more targeted and nuanced. It is not just "Jesus saves!" but "Jesus can help you deal with that addiction or that broken relationship, and here is how he can help." Some have argued that currently the main trend among Christians around the world is "religious modernization," a trend toward this-worldly religion more focused on helping people than on saving souls. But this analysis does not fit the Chinese situation. Chinese Christians eagerly proclaim that Jesus Christ is the way, the truth, and the life for this world and for the next.

Several pastors, when I asked about the strengths of their churches, responded with glowing praise for the purity and intensity of their parishioners' faith, for the depth and intensity of their parishioners' love for God and each other. Curiously, this was often combined with a lament about the shallowness of their biblical, theological knowledge. One rural pastor said he could easily recruit fifty people from his church to pray all night, but if they were asked to give a brief outline of the Christian faith, most could not do it. This lack of knowledge also helps to explain why cults are the number one problem for the church in China. In 2019, however, I saw some good improvements here. The pure and intense faith is still there, but it is accompanied by more depth, by a slow but steady growth in biblical and theological literacy.

Another strength of the registered church is its resilience, both as an organization and the individual believers who are part of it. They have weathered good times and bad, wealth and poverty. They have had to navigate their way through some of the most enormous changes that any society has ever gone through. Mostly, they have survived and flourished in the face of government pressure and opposition. They have also endured years of criticism from the unregistered church. And they have done all this with grace. After having dealt with the government for many decades, they know how to maneuver their way through almost any circumstance. Their ability to come up with alternate plans to whatever the government proposes is remarkable, as we've seen several times in this book.

Some pastors mentioned the growing involvement in social services as a strong point. Earlier, I described the Christian hospital in Luzhou and their programs for drug addicts. Another pastor brought up the example of churches in Yunnan and their treatment of people with AIDS and drug addictions. No doubt many more examples could be added. The increase in social action is part of a broader movement to understand the role of the church in society. Francis Khek Gee Lim, among others, argues that:

> For Christianity to establish itself even more firmly in Chinese culture, a Chinese Christian theology has to be developed based on empirical work that details the Christian communities' contemporary interpretation of their faith. To this end, some leaders and theologians in the official TSPM are reflecting critically about the role of the church in a rapidly changing society fraught with tensions and faced with huge challenges, and are actively discussing "Theological Reconstruction"[1] to enable the Christian church to maintain its relevance in society through greater social awareness and engagement.[2]

"Sinicization" has replaced "Theological Reconstruction," but other than that, Lim's assessment in 2013 is likely even more the case today. Pastors today are busy adopting what is good in the movement, like the use of Chinese songs in worship, the use of everyday Chinese experiences and stories as illustrations in sermons, the use of Chinese faces in art, and so on. At the same time, they are guarding and preaching against dangerous changes in theology through sermons that, although not always so riveting, are focused on scripture and present the gospel that has come down through the ages. Additionally, an encouraging strength of the registered churches is that recent graduates of schools like Jinling Seminary in Nanjing, Yanjing Seminary in Beijing, and Northeast Seminary in Shenyang exhibit much higher levels of theological, social, and emotional maturity than previously.

Another strength is less tangible, yet real. Chinese Christians have hope, hope for the present in spite of government pressure, and hope for the future. This hope is connected to a growing sense of institutional unity, making the bond between churches stronger. While hard to define or measure, this hope was evident in the words and manner of the pastors. This sense of hope is also tied, I believe, to a growing sense of unity among the pastors as well. Christ prayed fervently for his followers to be one (John 17:21). It is ironic that in some small way the atheistic Communist government's attempt to better control the church by consolidating it into one organization has helped to answer Christ's prayer. A Beijing pastor reminded me that while these were difficult times for the church and for society, the strength of the church is its hope and faith. Partially, this hope is based on the memory of how the church has survived, and even flourished, through periods of extreme persecution. Against all odds, the church has

---

1. The forerunner of Sinicization.
2. Lim, *Christianity in Contemporary China*, 6.

maintained its theological identity. Faries writes, describing the church in the early twenty-first century: "Despite government supervision and some politicization of the church structures, somehow the "official church" at the level of pastor, seminary student, and parishioner has remained conservative and evangelical, "merely" Christian, to borrow C.S. Lewis's phrase."[3]

My experience tells me that what Faries wrote in the early 2000s is still true in 2020. In fact, the conservative evangelical character of the church is even more solid now, and there continues to be hope for the future.

3. Faries, *The "Inscrutably Chinese" Church,* 263.

Conclusion

Journal Entry, June 18, 2011 Chengdu, Sichuan Province

On Sunday, my wife and I set out for a church service at one of Chengdu's largest churches. The worship service was supposed to start at ten o'clock. When we arrived, we found the doors closed. It turned out that a new church was being built, and during the process, members simply attended other churches. We found one of these churches called the *Enguang*, or Shining Grace Church. The church was started by a Canadian Methodist missionary in the late 1800s, and the building seemed probably as old. It is a brick structure in traditional twentieth-century American church architectural style, with wooden buttresses holding up the ceiling.

Singing practice was going on when we arrived. The church was comfortably full, probably eight hundred or so in attendance. The congregation was mostly seniors and middle-aged couples. Some things I noticed about this church: the singing was terrible, off key and off beat; people talked through the whole service, a constant background rumble; the choir was so quiet that I had to ask my wife, Lynn, if they were even singing; and balloons. I had been to services like this in many rural churches, so none of this was surprising. Except for the balloons; they were an inexplicable anomaly.

Pastor Zhang's sermon was rather standard fare on John 1, entitled "Jesus is the Son of God." The service order was traditional and included the Apostles Creed.

After the service, unable to track down Pastor Zhang, I talked with a retired Pastor Lu. He told me that the church has five services, with an attendance of about eight hundred at each, for a total of four thousand or so worshiping each week. The church has three pastors and two evangelists. He figured that the total number of believers in the registered churches in Chengdu was about 20,000, worshipping at the four churches in the city, a few more in the suburbs, and a number of meeting points. All these numbers seem low to me. When asked about the challenges facing the church, Pastor Lu said that the meeting points are not tied closely enough to the churches, some of them having no contact at all. He felt this easily leads to disorganization and the tendency to fall into heretical beliefs. In general, he felt there was not enough leadership training and therefore a lack of strong leadership. He made an interesting comment when asked about the strong points of the church. He said Christians now are self-motivated and self-reliant. They no longer rely on foreign missions and churches or on the government. They are more assertive.

After the takeover of China by the Communists in 1949, some Western missionaries and scholars predicted the death of the church in China, but instead there was rebirth on a scale never before seen. So, what about the next twenty-five years or so? Will there be similar surprises? If so, will they be good surprises or bad? What will happen with the church-State relationship? What about the relationship between the registered and unregistered churches? Will Sinicization be a positive or negative force? What will the next set of religious regulations be like?

I don't pretend to have answers or even educated guesses, but many pastors and religious leaders I interviewed offered their opinions, ranging from extremely positive and optimistic to suspicious and negative.

THE PASTORS WEIGH IN

The majority opinion regarding the future of the church in China is overwhelmingly hopeful. One pastor summed up the thoughts of many: "The future is full of glory, all because of God! The church has the same future as Jesus because it is the body of Christ." Another echoed with "The future of the church is bright!" And again, "Regarding the future of the church in China, everything is under God's control." Another expressed similar beliefs: "The future of Christianity in China is bright because there are so many Christians who are wholeheartedly pursuing their beliefs and so many pastors who are willing to sacrifice themselves." Another pastor said that the church should simply go about being the church by focusing on evangelism and purity of life and doctrine: "As for the future of the church, it is the responsibility of the church to preach the gospel to more and more people. We should work on making the church healthier—make it better and more pure." These sentiments were shared by a good 75 percent of the pastors I interviewed. The belief that God is in control and will protect the church is widespread, even in the face of all the challenges, restrictions, and foreboding signs.

Other pastors, however, see many problems ahead, the main one being the contentious relationship between unregistered churches, registered churches, and the government. One church leader offered what seems to me a too-simplistic path forward. He claimed that much would be resolved if only the unregistered churches would get up and register:

> The constitution guarantees religious freedom, so the church will continue to be free. The government is selective about which churches can register. But most do not register. Maybe the Three-Self will compel house churches to be part of the organization.

Several issues arise out of this statement. Does the pastor really have that much faith in the constitutional "guarantee" of freedom of religion? What substantial surety has this provided to date, and what makes this pastor think anything will be different in the future? Most pastors see clearly that the constitution is meaningful only in the most limited way, and that even today's highly circumscribed freedom of religion is not a certainty in the future. And furthermore, registering is not even an accessible option for so many churches. Most would agree that the government does officially invite all churches to register. But "officially" may be different from the reality. Most churches that have tried to register have found the paperwork alone strewn with bureaucratic roadblocks. And, of course, the biggest hurdle to registering is the fact that registering means putting your church under Three-Self, governmental supervision, a step that most unregistered churches will never take. And then finally, even when a church has been willing to abide by the regulations, the government often either drags its feet or disallows the application outright.

Many Christians in China are optimistic that as the church keeps growing, it will finally reach a critical mass, at which point it will have a significant amount of social and political influence. A corollary to this was brought up by a church member: "As more and more people go abroad to study or visit, they will have a better idea of what freedom is." Many pastors see that change will come from the young people. Their experiences with the internet, with foreign university professors, and with international travel are Pandora's boxes that can never be shut. Their curiosity and their quests for more freedom and for more self-determination could eventually translate into greater freedoms for their societies as well as for their churches.

Some leaders are more negative regarding the future of the church. One Beijing unregistered church member said that, "registered church growth in the future will level off. This is mainly because they are under the control of the Communist Party. In the future, Christian growth will continue, but mainly in small, unregistered meeting places." Along the same lines, a rural unregistered church member said, "The future of the registered church is not good. They are being choked by too many regulations. Registered churches are primarily in the city. The house church has broader inroads into all parts of society." Both of these commentators agree that the registered churches are under more government control and, therefore, under more pressure than their own churches. It cannot be denied that the government can more easily control the registered churches because they are visible and they already have organizational ties to the government. It also cannot be denied that if the government would determine to aggressively regulate unregistered churches, the results would be grave.

A Beijing pastor had a much more detailed, if somewhat rambling, opinion of the current church situation as well as its future. His opinions are worth quoting at length:

> The future of the church is hard to predict right now. Really dedicated Christians are hard to find. Very few are willing to give their lives for the Gospel. Everyone is out for themselves. If the churches don't cooperate, the church will have no future. The church is becoming like the world; it is losing its true faith. There are more "Christmas and Easter" Christians. Rural Christian faith is much more sincere. But the number of people in rural churches is decreasing. Everyone has moved to the city. In one sense, there are too many churches in the city. People claim that they have studied in "such-and-such" a place, then they start their own church and take all the offerings. Belief is seen as a way to get rich; they deceive the believers out of their money. Another problem is that there are not enough evangelists and the evangelists are not properly supported, especially in rural areas. Many evangelists are leaving the church. The ones that remain often just preach nonsense. They don't have time or energy to read the scriptures or pray. And in rural areas probably 70 percent of evangelists have not been trained in seminary.

Everyone I interviewed affirmed the shortage of trained evangelists and pastors, but only recently have I heard the disconcerting charges that charlatans are deceiving people out of their money and using the church to get rich. Even more serious are the charges that really dedicated and faithful Christians are hard to find. During the Cultural Revolution, the deep and unbreakable faith of the Christians kept the church alive. Now Christians are heading into another period of government interference and pressure that will test their faith in different ways. If, as this pastor argues, many Christians are simply selfish and shallow, then the church could be headed for disaster.

I am doubtful that things have reached this point. I see many positive signs that far outweigh the negatives expressed by this last pastor. Most pastors and leaders that I interviewed hold a more balanced and nuanced hope for the future of the church. I appreciate how one Beijing pastor shared his hope:

> As for the future, only God knows. But according to what we can know, there will be a lot of difficulty and challenges for the church. Satan will use all sorts of methods to tempt the church and use his influence to bring persecution on the church. But I am hopeful because the doors are not opened by people but by God. It is right that difficulties come because it is only when there are troubles that true faith can be seen. Since Beijing is the capital and a window to the government, the government has to be careful because everyone is watching. Because of that, the churches are protected. For the rest of the country, it is hard to say. A lot depends on what the government knows about a particular church and whether it is orthodox or not.

ORTHODOXY, ECCLESIOLOGY, AND THE FUTURE

Interestingly, the push for developing a uniquely Chinese Christian orthodoxy comes not from the churches themselves, but from the government. The State, actually, is demanding of the churches to "spell out" its orthodox stand. Why? This is an officially atheistic government, what does it care about religious orthodoxy? Apparently, plenty. Ever since the Communist government declared in its constitution that religious freedom would be limited to orthodox expressions of five religions, Buddhism, Daoism, Islam, Catholicism, and Protestant Christianity, government officials have been compelled to be able to identify the lines between orthodoxy and heterodoxy.

It is rather amusing to imagine a group of Communist Party officials sitting around a table involved in a deep discussion about whether a particular group, say Eastern Lightning, is orthodox or not. How would they know the appropriate scripture or history upon which to hang such a decision? Amusing or not, it is serious for the churches and other religious groups. The government's decision on orthodoxy determines the treatment the group receives, whether it is accepted or determined to be a cult and outlawed.

To this point, the focus on orthodoxy has not impacted the registered Protestant churches as they are almost by definition orthodox, but that could change. The government's push for Sinicization, some argue, is an attempt to marry traditional Christianity with traditional Chinese culture and modern socialist ideology. Would this lead to a new brand of Chinese Christianity that could very well produce a new orthodoxy? If this new orthodoxy included beliefs that were antithetical to Christianity, it would certainly be problematic for the church. The government does not seem to be moving in this direction at this point, but in China, things change quickly and unpredictably. The government will continue to ask for an orthodoxy that benefits the government. In many ways, the amazing thing is that the church has survived this long with its theology intact.

The government is not only concerned with theological orthodoxy. It is also making moves in the area of church ecclesiology or organization. While the Three-Self had been a movement promoting local Chinese leadership in the church in the areas of finance, outreach, and church governance, the government seems to be twisting it into an organ of State control, and now the State seems to be doing something similar with the meeting points. The relationship between large churches and their meeting points has always been one of y*itang daidian,* that is, one in which the large churches are responsible for the meeting points. Most meeting points originated from large churches that helped them procure their building and provided interim pastors and evangelists to preach and supervise the sacraments. This structure, however, has traditionally been one of support rather than supervision. It was most primarily an arrangement that helped the handicapped, the elderly, and the infirm, as well as those who lived too far away from a large church. The new regulations, however, emphasize that the large churches are expected to supervise and be responsible for the behavior of the meeting points. One pastor described it this way:

> The meeting points can be large or small, they may or may not have a pastor, or they may meet in homes or in rented places. But they need to recognize that they are under the authority of the large church. Also, groups like the local police and "peacekeepers" are involved in keeping watch over the meeting points. So, they will ask questions like: "How many people attend?" "What are you doing?" "What sorts of people are attending?" "Who is preaching or teaching?" So, things are now more restricted. Also, the "street patrol" will keep their eyes open for

unregistered church meetings and report those to the police. Sometimes people need to show their ID when they enter the church, and it is noted whether you are a local resident or a transient. This is only at the meeting points for now, not at the big church.

What had been a voluntary association is now an official method of control. An informal arrangement that benefitted the meeting points is being changed into a formal, government-mandated structure. In effect, the large churches are now responsible for policing the meeting points. As one pastor said, "It is easier to control one large church than one hundred small ones."

Much of the literature and reporting on the church in China has to do in one way or another with State control of religion. This refers of course to control of churches or other religious groups. It is an organizational approach to control. But lately, the State is interested in something else, something more. Recently, the State is moving into the area of personal control. China's Orwellian ranking of citizens by means of a social credit system, combined with its use of facial recognition software, has allowed the government to begin to exert control on the personal level.[1] While still in its infancy, this new technology has horrific possibilities. And it could be used against personal belief. Imagine being given negative points for attending church or Bible study, or for having Christian friends, negative points that eventually could cause you to lose your passport or your job. We've already heard of situations like this. Can expanded use of this technological power be far behind? If the State can control individuals, making it difficult to impossible to be involved in church, it will not need to control the churches; they will die of attrition.

Now at the end of 2019, the tension in the air is palpable, and the sense of foreboding is strong. Chinese Christians of all types feel it. Some have suffered and more likely will. The State seems highly motivated and well prepared to do battle with the church. Cultural Revolution-like scenarios are not a certainty, but cannot be ruled out. The church, however, is also ready. In all my interviews, I sensed no fear. Instead, there was a conviction that God would watch over his people. There was a substantive faith of the type that moves mountains. As so many pastors said, the church in China is God's church, and he will take care of it.

---

1. ChinaSource Team, "Facial Recognition and the Church."

Appendix

Religious Affairs Regulations

Translation by China Law Translate

Text quoted from https://www.chinalawtranslate.com/en/
religious-affairs-regulations-2017/.

August 1, 2020

CONTENTS

CHAPTER I: GENERAL PROVISIONS

Article 1

These Regulations are formulated in accordance with the Constitution and relevant laws so as to ensure citizens' freedom of religious belief, maintain harmony among and between religions, maintain social harmony, regulate the administration of religious affairs, and increase the level of legalification in work on religion.

Article 2

Citizens have the freedom of religious belief.

No organization or individual may compel citizens to believe in, or not to believe in, any religion; nor may they discriminate against citizens who believe in any religion (hereinafter referred to as religious citizens) or citizens who do not believe in any religion (hereinafter referred to as non-religious citizens).

Religious citizens and non-religious citizens shall respect each other and co-exist in harmony, and so shall citizens who believe in different religions.

Article 3

The management of religious affairs upholds the principles of protecting what is lawful, prohibiting what is unlawful, suppressing extremism, resisting infiltration, and fighting crime.

Article 4

The State, in accordance with the law, protects normal religious activities,actively guides religion to fit in with socialist society, and safeguards the lawful rights and interests of religious groups, religious schools, religious activity sites and religious citizens.

Religious groups, religious schools, religious activity sites, and religious citizens shall abide by the Constitution, laws, regulations and rules; practice the core socialist values; and preserve the unification of the country, ethnic unity, religious harmony and social stability.

Religion must not be used by any individual or organization to engage in activities that endanger national security, disrupt public order, impair the health of citizens or obstruct the State educational system, as well as other activities that harm State or societal public interests, or citizens' lawful rights and interests, and other such illegal activities.

Individuals and organizations must not create contradictions and conflicts between different religions, within a single religion, or between religious and non-religious citizens; must not advocate, support, or fund, religious extremism; and must not use religion to undermine ethnic unity, divide the nation or carry out terrorist activities.

Article 5

All religions shall adhere to the principle of independence and self-governance; religious groups, religious schools, and religious activity sites and religious affairs, are not to be controlled by foreign forces.

Religious bodies, religious schools, religious activity sites, and religious professionals are to develop external exchange on the basis of mutual respect, equality, and friendship; other organizations or individuals must not accept any religious conditions in external cooperation or exchange in economic, cultural or other fields.

Article 6

All levels of people's government shall strengthen work on religion, establish and complete mechanisms for work on religion, and ensure the strength of and the necessary conditions for the work.

The religious affairs departments of the people's governments at the county level or above are to lawfully carry out management of religious affairs that involve State or public interests, and the other departments of the people's governments at the county level or above are to be responsible for the management of relevant affairs within the scope of their respective functions and duties.

People's governments at the township level shall complete efforts for the management of religious affairs within their own administrative areas. Villagers' committees and residents' committees shall lawfully assist people's governments in managing religious affairs.

All levels of people's governments shall hear the views of religious groups, religious schools, religious activity sites, and religious citizens, and coordinate the management of religious affairs so as to provide public services to religious groups, religious schools and religious activity sites.

CHAPTER II: RELIGIOUS GROUPS

Article 7

The establishment, modification, or deregistration of a religious group shall be registered in accordance with the relevant State provisions on the management of social groups.

The charters of religious groups shall comply with the relevant State provisions on the management of social groups.

Activities carried out by religious groups in accordance with their charters are protected by law.

Article 8

Religious groups have the following functions:

1. Assisting the people's governments in the implementation of laws, regulations, rules, and policies, to preserve the lawful rights and interests of religious citizens;

2. Guiding religious affairs, formulating a system of rules and supervising their implementation;

3. Engaging in religious cultural study, explaining the religious doctrines and canons, and carrying out the construction of religious ideology;

4. Carrying out religious education and training, cultivating religious professionals, and designating and managing religious professionals;

5. Such other functions as laws, regulations, rules and religious groups' articles of association provide.

Article 9

National religious groups and those of the provinces, autonomous regions, and directly-governed municipalities may, based on the need of their respective religions, select and receive religious students studying overseas in accordance with provisions; other organizations or individuals must not select and accept religious students studying overseas.

Article 10

Religious schools, religious activity sites, and religious professionals shall abide by the rules formulated by religious groups.

CHAPTER III: RELIGIOUS SCHOOLS

Article 11

Religious schools are established by national religious groups or by the religious groups of provinces, autonomous regions, and directly-governed municipalities. Other organizations or individuals must not establish religious schools.

Article 12

The establishment of religious schools shall be by upon application of the national religious groups to the religious affairs department under the State Council, of application of the religious groups of provinces, autonomous regions, directly-governed municipalities to the departments religious affairs for the people's government of that province, autonomous region, or directly-governed municipalities. The religious affairs departments of provincial, autonomous region, or directly governed municipality people's governments shall make a recommendation within 30 days of receiving the application; and report to the department of religious affairs under the State Council.

The religious affairs department under the State Council shall make a decision to approve or not approve within 60 days of receiving a national religious group's application, or the report materials from the religious affairs departments of people's governments for provinces, autonomous regions, or directly-governed municipalities.

Article 13

Religious schools shall meet the following conditions to be established:

1. Have clear training objectives, school regulations, and curriculum plans;

2. Have a source of students that meet the requirements for training;

3. Have the necessary school funding and stable sources of funds;

4. Have teaching sites, facilities, and equipment necessary for the pedagogic mission and teaching model;

5. Have a full-time responsible party for the school, qualified full-time teachers, and internal management organizations.

6. A reasonable configuration.

Article 14

Religious schools established upon approval may apply to register as legal persons in accordance with relevant provisions.

Article 15

Religious schools shall follow the provisions of article 12 of these regulations in handling changes of their addresses, school names, affiliations, training objectives, education systems, or school sizes, or where merging, dividing, or terminating.

Article 16

Religious schools are to carry out designated systems for verification of teachers' qualifications, review of titles, and giving of degrees; with specific measures separately formulated by the department of religious affairs under the State Council.

Article 17

Religious schools hiring foreign professional staff shall do so after the State Council religious affairs department consents, and go to the department for administration of foreign workers for their area to handle the relevant formalities.

Article 18

Religious groups and temples, Taoist temples, mosques, and churches (hereinafter temples and churches), carrying out religious education and training to cultivate religious professionals where the training period is 3 months or more, shall hall report for review and approval to the religious affairs departments of local people's governments at the districted city level or higher.

Chapter IV: Religious Activity Sites

Article 19

Religious activity sites include temples and churches and other fixed locations for religious activity.

Standards for distinguishing temples and churches and other fixed sites for religious premises are to be formulated by the religious affairs departments of provincial, autonomous region, or directly governed municipality people's governments, and reported to the religious affairs department under the State Council to be filed for the record.

Article 20

Religious activity sites shall meet the following conditions to be established:

1. The purpose of their establishment is not contrary to articles 4 and 5 of this Regulation;

2. The local religious citizens have need to regularly conduct collective religious activities;

3. There are religious professionals or other personnel meeting the requirements of the religion who intend to preside over the religious activities;

4. Have the necessary funds from legal sources and channels;

5. Have a reasonable configuration meeting the requirements of urban and rural planning, and not impeding the ordinary lives and production of surrounding units and residents.

Article 21

In preparation for the establishment of a religious activity site, religious groups are to submit applications to the religious affairs department of the county-level people's governments for the area where the religious activity site will be. Within 30 days of religious affairs departments of county-level people's governments receiving an application; they shall report to the religious affairs department of districted cities' people's government.

Religious affairs departments for districted city level people's governments shall, within 30 days of receiving reported materials from a county-level people's governments' religious affairs department, make a decision to approve or reject give approval or reject applications to establish other fixed religious activity sites; where the application is for the establishment of temples and churches, it shall issue verification comments and report to the religious affairs department of the provincial, autonomous region, or directly governed municipality people's government for review and approval.

The religious affairs department of provincial, autonomous region, or directly governed municipality people's governments shall make a decision to approve or not approve within 30 days of receiving the report materials from the religious affairs departments of people's governments for districted cities.

Only after an application for the establishment of a religious activity site has been approved, may preparations to build the religious activity site be handled.

Article 22

After religious activity sites have been approved for preparations and completed construction, they shall apply for registration with the religious affairs department of the county-level people's government for that area. Religious affairs departments of county-level people's governments shall, within 30 days of receiving an application, conduct a review of the religious activity site's management organization and regulatory system, and issue a "Religious Activity Site Registration Certificate."

Article 23

Religious activity sites meeting the requirements for legal personhood, may register as legal persons with the civil affairs departments upon the consent of an area religious group and reporting to the religious affairs department of a County Level people's government for review and consent.

Article 24

Where religious activity sites terminate or modify the content of their registration, they shall handle the formalities corresponding to the cancellation or modification of registration with the original registration management organ.

Article 25

Religious activity sites shall establishment management organizations and implement democratic management. The members of religious activity sites' management organizations are selected according to democratic consultation, and are reported to that site's registration management organs to be filed for the record.

Article 26

Religious activity sites shall strengthen internal management, and follow relevant laws, regulations and rules to establish and complete systems for the management of personnel, finances, assets, accounting, security, fire protection, protection of relics, health and disease prevention and so forth; and will accept the guidance, supervision and inspection of relevant departments of the local people's governments.

Article 27

Religious affairs departments shall conduct oversight and inspections of religious activity sites' compliance with laws, regulations, and rules; the establishment and implementation of site management systems; the modification of registration matters; as well as religious activities and activities involving foreign entities. Religious activity sites shall accept oversight and inspections from religious affairs departments.

Article 28

Religious goods, crafts, and publications may be sold within religious activity sites.

Article 29

Religious activity sites shall guard against incidents that harm the religious sentiment of religious citizens, undermine ethnic unity, and influence social stability, such as the occurrence of major accidents on the premises or violation of religious taboos.

When the incidents or matters listed in the preceding paragraph occur, religious activity sites shall immediately report them to the religious affairs department of the county-level people's government for that area.

Article 30

Religious groups, temples and churches intending to build large outdoor religious statues shall have provincial, autonomous region, or directly governed municipality religious groups submit an application to the religious affairs department of a provincial, autonomous region, or directly governed municipality people's governments. The religious affairs departments of provincial, autonomous region, or directly governed municipality people's governments shall make a recommendation within 30 days of receiving the application; and report to the department of religious affairs under the State Council.

The religious affairs department under the State Council shall make a decision to approve or not approve within 60 days of receiving a report on the construction of a large outdoor religious statue.

Organizations and individuals other than religious groups, temples and churches must not construct large outdoor religious statues.

The construction of large outdoor religious statues outside of temple and church grounds is prohibited.

Article 31

Relevant units and individuals setting up commercial service outlets, organizing displays and exhibitions, or filming movies and television, and carrying out other activities in religious activity sites, shall first obtain the consent of the religious activity sites.

Article 32

All levels of local people's government shall include the establishment of religious activity sites in their land use plans and urban-rural planning, based on actual needs.

The construction of religious activity sites and large outdoor religious statues shall conform with overall land use plans, urban-rural plans, and relevant laws and regulations such as on engineering, construction and preservation of artifacts.

Article 33

Reconstruction or construction of new buildings in religious activity sites shall be done after approval by the religious affairs department of a local people's government at the county level or above, and then handling formalities such as for planning and construction.

Expansion of religious activity sites, or rebuilding in different locations, should be handled in accordance with the procedures provided in article 21 of these Regulations.

Article 34

Where there are religious activity sites in scenic areas, local people's governments at the county level or above shall coordinate and handle interests and relationships between the religious activity sites and scenic area management organizations, in areas such as gardens, forestry, cultural relics, tourism and so forth, to preserve the lawful rights and interests of religious activity sites, religious professionals, and religious citizens, and to protect normal religious activities.

The planning and construction of scenic areas with religious activity sites as the primary sightseeing attraction, shall be coordinated with the style and environment of the religious activity sites.

Article 35

Where religious citizens need to regularly conduct collective religious activities, but don't possess the conditions for applying to set up religious activity sites, a representative of the religious citizens is to submit an application to the religious affairs department of the county-level people's government, and after the religious affairs department for the county-level people's government solicits the opinions of local religious groups and township-level people's governments, it may designate a temporary activity site for them.

Under the guidance of the religious affairs departments of county-level people's governments, township-level people's governments conduct oversight of activities at temporary activity locations. After they possess the conditions for setting up religious activity sites, reviews, approvals and registration formalities for establishing religious activity sites are to be completed.

Religious activities at temporary activity sites shall comply with the relevant provisions of these Regulations.

CHAPTER V: RELIGIOUS PROFESSIONALS

Article 36

Upon affirmation by a religious group and reporting to the religious affairs department of a people's government at the county level or above to be filed for the record, religious professionals may engage in professional religious activities.

The succession of living Buddhas in Tibetan Buddhism is to be conducted under the guidance of Buddhist groups and in accordance with the religious rites and historical conventions, and is to be reported for approval to the religious affairs department of people's governments at the provincial level or above or to a people's government at the provincial level or above. The national Catholic religious group is to report Catholic bishops to the religious affairs department under the State Council to be filed for the record.

Those that have not obtained or have lost religious professional credentials, must not engage in activity as religious professionals.

Article 37

Where religious professionals serve or depart as the chief religious professionals of religious activity sites, upon consent of that religion's religious group, it is to be reported to the religious affairs department of the people's government at the county level or above for the record.

Article 38

Religious professionals presiding over religious activities, conducting religious ceremonies, sorting religious scriptures and conducting of religious and cultural research, and carrying out public interest charitable activities and other such activities, are protected by law.

Article 39

Religious professionals lawfully participate in social security and enjoy the corresponding rights. Religious groups, religious schools, and religious activity sites shall handle social insurance registration for religious professionals in accordance with provisions.

CHAPTER VI: RELIGIOUS ACTIVITIES

Article 40

Collective religious activities of religious citizens shall , in general, be held at religious activity sites, be organized by religious activity sites, religious groups, or religious school organizations; and be presided over by religious professionals or other persons meeting the requirements of that religion's rules; and conducted according to religious doctrines and canons.

Article 41

Non-religious groups, non-religious schools, non-religious activity sites, or non-designated temporary activity sites must not hold religious activities, must not accept religious donations.

Non-religious groups, non-religious schools, and non-religious activity sites, must not carry out religious training and must not organize citizens leaving the country to participate in religious training, meetings, activities and so forth.

Article 42

Where a large-scale religious activity, which crosses-provinces, autonomous regions and directly governed municipalities is held that is beyond the accommodation capacity of a religious activity site, or where a large-scale religious activity is to be held outside a religious activities site, the religious group, church or temple sponsoring the activity shall, 30 days before the activity is to be held, submit an application to the religious affairs department of the people's government for the province, autonomous region or municipality The religious affairs department of the people's government for districted cities shall, within 15 days from the date of receiving an application, is to make a decision of approval or disapproval after soliciting the opinions of the public security organs for that level of people's government. Where a decision to approve is made, the approving organ is to record it with the provincial level people's government's religious affairs department.

Large-scale religious activities shall, as required indicated in the written notification of approval, to proceed in accordance with religious rites and rituals, and must not violate the relevant provisions of Articles 4 and 5 of these Regulations. The sponsoring religious group or church or temple shall employ effective measures to prevent the occurrence of accidents and guarantee that large-scale religious activities are conducted safely and orderly. The township-level people's government and the relevant departments of the local people's government at the county level or above for the place where such large-scale religious activities are to be held shall, within the limits of their respective functions and duties, carry out the necessary management and guidance.

Article 43

The national Islamic religious group is responsible for the making of hajj abroad by Chinese citizens who believe in Islam.

Article 44

It is prohibited to proselytize, hold religious activities, establish religious organizations, or set up religious activity sites in schools or educational bodies other than religious schools.

Article 45

Religious groups, religious schools, and churches and temples may, in accordance with the relevant national provisions, compile and distribute internal religious informational publications. Religious publications for public distribution are to be handled in accordance with the relevant national provisions on the administration of publications.

Publications involving religious contents shall comply with laws and regulations on the administration of publications, and must not contain the following content:

1. That which undermines the harmonious co-existence between religious and non-religious citizens;

2. That which undermines the harmony between different religions or within a religion;

3. That which discriminates against or insults religious or non-religious citizens;

4. That which advocate religious extremism;

5. That which contravenes the principle of religions' independence and self-governance.

Article 46

Religious publications or printed matter that exceeds personal use and reasonable quantities brought into the mainland, or otherwise imported, shall be handled in accordance with relevant state regulations.

Article 47

Engagement in internet religious information services shall be upon the review and consent of the religious affairs department for a people's governments at the provincial level or above, and handle it in accordance with the relevant state provisions on internet information services management.

Article 48

Information on internet religious information services shall comply with relevant laws, regulations,and rule' relevant provisions on the management of religious affairs.

Internet religious information services' content must not violate the provisions of paragraph 2 of article 45 of these Regulations.

CHAPTER VII: RELIGIOUS ASSETS

Article 49

Religious groups, religious schools, and religious activity sites follow laws and relevant state provisions to manage and use assets that they lawfully occupy and that are collectively owned assets belonging to the State; and enjoy ownership or other property rights with regards to other lawful assets in accordance with law.

Article 50

Religious groups', religious schools', and religious activity sites' lawful use of land; lawful ownership or use of buildings, structures, and facilities, as well as of other lawful assets and proceeds; are protected by law.

The lawful assets of a religious groups, religious schools or religious activities sites must not be encroached upon, plundered, privately divided, damaged, or, illegally sealed up, seized, frozen, confiscated or disposed of by any organization or individual, and cultural relics possessed or used by religious groups, religious schools, or religious activities sites must not be damaged.

Article 51

Immovable property such as the houses owned and the land used by religious groups, religious schools, or religious activities sites shall be registered on application with the real estate registration institution for the people's government at the county level or above in accordance with law, and be granted a real estate ownership certificate; where the property rights are modified or transferred, the formalities for alteration or transfer of registration shall be promptly handled

When altering or transferring the land-use rights of a religious group, religious school, or a religious activities site, the real estate registration institutions shall solicit the opinions of the religious affairs department of the people's government at the same level.

Article 52

Religious groups, religious schools, and religious activity sites are non-profit organizations; their assets and income shall be used in activities consistent with their religious purpose and in public interest charitable matters, and they must not distributed.

Article 53

Organizations and individuals that give donations for the construction of religious activity sites do not enjoy ownership or usage rights in the religious activity sites, and must not receive economic benefit from the religious activity sites.

It is prohibited to invest in or contract management of religious activity sites or large-scale outdoor religious statues, and it is prohibited to commercial promotions in the name of religions.

Article 54

The houses and structures used for religious activities by a religious activities site, as well as their accessory houses lived in by religious professionals must not be transferred, mortgaged or used as investments in kind.

Article 55

Where the houses of a religious group, religious school, or a religious activities site need to be demolished due to the needs of the public interest, it shall be done in accordance with the national laws and regulations on demolition of houses. Religious groups, religious schools, or religious activity sites may elect monetary compensation, and may also select exchange of real estate rights or reconstruction.

Article 56

Religious groups, religious schools, religious activity sites, and religious professionals may lawfully initiate public interest charitable endeavors.

Public interest charitable activities must not be used to proselytize by any organization or individual.

Article 57

Religious groups, religious schools or religious activities sites may, in accordance with the relevant national provisions, accept donations from organizations and individuals at home or abroad, which shall be used for the activities that are commensurate with the purpose of the religious group or the religious activities site.

Religious groups, religious schools, and religious activity sites must not accept donations from foreign organizations or individuals that have conditions attached, and where the amount donated exceeds 100,000 RMB; it shall be reported to the religious affairs department of the people's governments at the county level or above for review and approval.

Religious groups, religious schools, and religious activity sites may accept contributions from citizens in accordance with religious custom, but contributions must not be compelled or levied.

Article 58

Religious groups, religious schools or religious activities sites shall implement the national unified systems for finance, assets, and accounting, and report to the religious affairs department of the people's government at the county level or above for the place where it is located on its income and expenditure, and on the acceptance and use of donations as well, and, in an appropriate way, make such information public to religious citizens. The religious affairs departments shall share relevant information with the relevant departments.

Religious groups, religious schools or religious activities sites shall, in accordance with national systems on finances and accounting, establish and complete systems audits, financial reporting, financial disclosures, and other such systems; and establish and improve financial management bodies, and allot the necessary financial accounting staff to strengthen financial management.

The relevant government departments may organize finance and asset inspections, and audits of religious groups, religious schools, and religious activity sites.

Article 59

Religious groups, religious schools, and religious activity sites shall handle tax registrations for religious professionals in accordance with law.

Religious groups, religious schools, religious activity sites, and religious professionals shall lawfully handle tax declarations, and enjoy tax benefits in accordance with relevant state provisions.

Tax departments shall lawfully implement taxation management for religious groups, religious schools, religious activity sites, and religious professionals.

Article 60

Where religious groups, religious schools, and religious activity sites are deregistered or terminated, an asset liquidation shall be carried out, and assets remaining after the liquidation shall be used for purposes conforming to their religious purpose.

CHAPTER VIII: LEGAL RESPONSIBILITY

Article 61

Where state personnel in the management of religious affairs abuse their authority, play favorites, neglects his duty or commits illegalities for personal gain, they shall be punished in accordance with law; where a crime is constituted, criminal responsibility is pursued in accordance with law.

Article 62

Where citizens are compelled to believe in, or not to believe in religion, or where normal religious activities conducted by a religious group, religious school or a religious activities site are interfered with, the religious affairs department is to order corrections; where there are violations of public security management, public security administrative sanctions are to be given in accordance with law.

Where the lawful rights and interests of a religious group, religious school, religious activities site or a religious citizen are infringed, civil liability is born in accordance with law; where a crime is constituted, criminal responsibility is pursued in accordance with law.

Article 63

Advocating, supporting, or funding religious extremism, or using religion to harm national security or public safety, undermine ethnic unity, divide the nation, or conduct terrorist activities and separatism or terrorist activities, infringing upon citizens' rights in their persons and democratic rights, impeding the administration of public order, or encroaching upon public or private property; where a crime is constituted, criminal responsibility is pursued in accordance with law; where no crime is constituted, the relevant competent department are to give administrative punishments in accordance with law; and where losses are caused to citizens, legal persons or other organizations, civil liability in borne in accordance with law.

Where religious groups, religious schools or religious activity sites carry out any of the conduct in the preceding paragraph and the circumstances are serious, the relevant departments shall employ necessary measures to rectify it, and those refusing rectification are to have their registration certificate or establishment permit revoked in accordance with law by the registration management organs or organ that approved establishment.

Article 64

Where there are situations in the course of large scale religious activities that endanger national security or public safety, or seriously undermine public order, the relevant departments are to handle it and give punishments in accordance with laws and regulations; where the primary organizing religious group, temple or church bears responsibility, the registration management organ shall order them to withdraw and change the principle responsible person, and where circumstances are serious, the registration management organs are to revoke registration certificates.

Where large scale religious activities are organized without authorization, the religious affairs department together with the relevant departments are to order that the activities be stopped, and may give a concurrent fine of between 100,000 and 300,000 yuan; and where there are unlawful gains or illegal assets, confiscate them. Of these, where large scale religious activities are organized without authorization by religious groups or religious activity sites, the registration management organs may also order that religious group or religious activity site to withdraw and change the directly responsible management personnel.

Article 65

Where a religious group, religious school, or religious activities site commits any of the following acts, the religious affairs department is to order it to make corrections; where the circumstances are relatively serious, the registration management organ, or organ that that approved establishment, is to order the religious group, religious school, or the religious activities site to dismiss and replace the directly responsible; management personnel and where the circumstances are serious, the registration management organ, or organ that that approved establishment, is to order that daily activities be stopped, that management organizations be reorganized, and a period of rectification; where rectification is refused, the registration certificate or establishment permits are revoked in accordance with law; and where there are unlawful gains or illegal assets, they are to be confiscated:

1. Failing to follow the registration modification or recording formalities;

2. Religious schools violating the requirements of their training objectives, school regulations, and course setup;

3. Religious activities sites violating Article 16 of these Regulations, by failing to formulate relevant management systems, or failing to have management systems meet the requirements;

4. Religious activity sites violating article 54 of these provisions by transferring, mortgaging, or investing buildings, structures and living quarters for religious professionals;

5. Failing to promptly report the occurrence of major accidents or incidents in a religious activities site, and causing serious consequences;

6. Contravening the principle of religions' independence and self-governance in violation of the provisions of Article 5 of these Regulations;

7. Violating national regulations in accepting domestic or foreign donations;

8. Refusing to accept supervision and management lawfully carried out by the administrative management organs.

Article 66

Where activities in temporary activity sites violate the relevant provisions of these Regulations, the religious affairs department is to order corrections; where the circumstances are serious, they are to order a stop to the activities and revoke the temporary activity site; where there are unlawful gains or illegal assets, they are to be confiscated.

Article 67

Where religious groups, religious schools and religious activity sites violate the relevant management provisions on finances, accounting, assets and taxation, departments of finance, taxation and so forth will give punishments in accordance with the relevant provisions; where the circumstances are serious, upon proposal by the finance and taxation departments, the registration management organs, or organ that approved establishment, are to lawfully revoke registration certificate or establishment permits.

Article 68

Where any publications or internet religious information services involving religious content contain content prohibited by the second paragraph of Article 45 of these Regulations, the relevant departments are to impose administrative punishments upon the relevant responsible units and persons in accordance with law; and where a crime is constituted, criminal responsibility is pursued in accordance with law.

Where internet religious information services are engaged in without authorization or where services are provided exceeding the scope of an approved and recorded project, the relevant departments handle it in accordance with relevant laws and regulations.

Article 69

Where a religious activities site is established without authorization, or where a religious activity sites site that has had its registration revoked or registration certificate cancelled continues to carry out religious activities, or where a religious school is established without authorization, the religious affairs department, together with the relevant departments are to shut it down and confiscate the unlawful gains or illegal assets if any; where the unlawful gains or illegal assets cannot be determined, a fine of up to 50,000 yuan is imposed; the illegal houses or structures, if any, shall be disposed of by the planning and construction departments in accordance with law; and where there is conduct in violation of public security management, a public security administrative sanction is be imposed in accordance with law:

Where a non-religious group, non-religious school, non-religious activity site, or site not designated for temporary activities organizes or holds religious activities or accepts religious donations, the religious affairs department, together with the departments for public security, civil affairs, construction, education, culture, tourism, cultural artifacts, and so forth, will order it to discontinue the activities and will confiscate the unlawful gains and illegal assets, if any; and may give a fine of between one and three times the value of unlawful gains; where it is not possible to determine the unlawful gains,a fine of up to 50,000 RMB is given; and where a crime is constituted, criminal responsibility is pursued in accordance with law.

Article 70

Where, without authorization, religious citizens are organized to leave the mainland to participate in religious trainings, meetings,the hajj or other such activities, or religious education and training is carried out without authorization, the religious affairs department, together with the relevant departments, is to order it to discontinue the activities, may impose a concurrent fine of between 20,000 and 200,000 yuan, and is to confiscate the unlawful gains, if any; where a crime is constituted, criminal responsibility is pursued in accordance with law.

Where there is proselytization, organizing of religious activities, establishment of religious organizations, or establishment of religious activity sites in schools or educational institutions other than religious schools; the organ of review and approval or other relevant departments are to order corrections to be made within a certain time and give warnings; where there are unlawful gains, they are to be confiscated; where there circumstances are serious, order that enrollment is to be stopped and cancel education permits; and where a crime is constituted, criminal responsibility is pursued in accordance with law.

Article 71

Where conditions are provided for unlawful religious activities religious activities, the religious affairs departments are to give a warning and confiscate the unlawful gains or illegal assets, if any; where the circumstances are serious, a fine of between 20,000 and 200,000 yuan is to be imposed; where there are illegal buildings or structures, they are to be disposed of by the departments for planning and construction in accordance with law; and where there is conduct in violation of public security management, a public security administrative sanction is be given by in accordance with law.

Article 72

Where these Regulations are violated by constructed large scale outdoor religious statues, the religious affairs department together with the departments for land, planning, construction, tourism and so forth, are to order that work be stopped, and demolished within a set time; and confiscate unlawful gains if any; where circumstances are serious, a fine of between 5–10% of the construction costs is imposed.

Where there is investment in or contracting of operations of religious activity sites or large outdoor religious statues, the religious affairs department together with departments for industry and commerce, planning, construction, and so forth will order corrections and confiscate unlawful gains ; where the circumstances are serious, the registration management organs will revoke the religious activity site's registration certificates, and investigate the responsibility of relevant parties.

Article 73

Where religious professionals exhibit any of the following conduct, the Religious Affairs Department will give a warning, confiscate unlawful gains and confiscate illegal assets; where the circumstances are serious, the Religious Affairs Department will recommend that the relevant religious group, religious school or religious activity sites temporarily stop them from presiding over religious affairs activities or revoke their status as religious professionals; and pursue the responsibility of the relevant religious group, religious school, or religious activity sites' responsible party, and where there is conduct in violation of public security management,e a public security administrative sanction is given in accordance with law; and where a crime is constituted, criminal responsibility is pursued in accordance with law:

1. Advocating, supporting, or funding religious extremism, undermining ethnic unity, dividing the nation, and conducting terrorist activities, or participating in related activities;

2. Accepting domination by external forces, accepting clergy from foreign religious groups or organizations without authorization, as well as otherwise going against the principle of religious independence and self-governance;

3. Violating national regulations in accepting domestic or foreign donations;

4. Organizing, or presiding over unapproved religious activities held outside of religious activity sites;

5. Other acts in violation of laws, regulations, or rules.

Article 74

Where anyone impersonates religious professionals to carry out illegal acts such as conducting professional religious activities or defrauding funds, the religious affairs departments are to order it that the activities be discontinued; and confiscate the unlawful gains and illegal assets, if any; and give a concurrent fine of up to 10,000 yuan; where there are violations of public security, public security administrative sanctions are given in accordance with law; and where a crime is constituted, criminal responsibility is pursued in accordance with law.

Article 75

Where anyone is dissatisfied with administrative acts taken by the religious affairs departments, they may lawfully apply for an administrative reconsideration; where dissatisfied with the decision of the administrative reconsideration, they may lawfully raise an administrative lawsuit.

CHAPTER IX: SUPPLEMENTARY PROVISIONS

Article 76

Religious exchanges between the mainland and Hong Kong SAR, Macao SAR, and Taiwan, are handled in accordance with relevant laws, administrative regulations, and relevant national provisions.

Article 77

This Regulation shall become effective on February 1, 2018.

Bibliography

Ashiwa, Yoshiko, and David L. Wank, eds. *Making Religion, Making the State: The Politics of Religion in Modern China*. Stanford: Stanford University Press, 2009.

Bays, Daniel H. *A New History of Christianity in China*. Hoboken, NJ: Wiley-Blackwell, 2012.

Bennett, William. "Where Did Eastern Lightning Come From?" *ChinaSource* (blog), April 16, 2014. https://www.chinasource.org/resource-library/articles/where-did-eastern-lightning-come-from/.

Carpenter, Joel A., and Kevin R. den Dulk, eds. *Christianity in Chinese Public Life*. London: Palgrave Macmillan, 2014.

Chen, Jing. "Reconciliation is Good, But . . ." *ChinaSource* (blog), May 6, 2019. https://www.chinasource.org/resource-library/blog-entries/reconciliation-is-good-but/.

Chen, Shengfeng. "The Pastor's Identity." *ChinaSource* (blog), November 5, 2019. https://www.chinasource.org/resource-library/chinese-church-voices/the-pastors-identity/.

ChinaSource Team. "Chinese Church Voices: Concerns of a Three-Self Pastor for 2020." *ChinaSource*, March 24 and 31, 2020. https://www.chinasource.org/resource-library/chinese-church-voices/concerns-of-a-three-self-pastor-for-2020/.

———. "Cult Activity in China Impacts Churches." *China Church Voices*, May 19, 2019. https://www.chinasource.org/resource-library/chinese-church-vocies/cult-activity-in-china-impacts-churches/.

———. "Facial Recognition and the Church." *ChinaSource* (blog), December 24, 2019. https://www.chinasource.org/resource-library/chinese-church-voices/facial-recognition-and-the-church/.

———. "Left-Behind Children and the Rural Church." *ChinaSource* (blog), March 19, 2019. https://www.chinasource.org/resource-library/chinese-church-vocies/left-behind-children-and-the-rural-church/.

Coulson, Gail V. *The Enduring Church: Christians in China and Hong Kong*. New York: Friendship, 1996.

Dunch, R. "Christianity and 'Adaptation to Socialism.'" In *Chinese Religiosities: Afflictions of Modernity and State Formation*, edited by M. Y. Yang, 155–78. Berkeley: University of California Press, 2008.

Esherick, Joseph. *The Origins of The Boxer Uprising*. Berkeley: University of California Press, 1987.

Falkenstine, Mike. *The Chinese Puzzle: Putting the Pieces Together for a Deeper Understanding of China and Her Church*. Longwood, FL: Xulon, 2008.

Fiedler, Katrin. "The Emergence of Christian Subcultures in China." In *Christianity in Contemporary China*, edited by Francis Khek Gee Lim, 138–52. New York: Routledge, 2013.

Fulton, Brent. *China's Urban Christians: A Light that Cannot Be Hidden*. Studies in Chinese Christianity. Eugene, OR: Pickwick Publications, 2015.

———. "The Challenge of Contextualization: Another Perspective." *ChinaSource* (blog), May 30, 2018. https://www.chinasource.org/resource-library/blog-entries/the-challenge-of-contextualization/.

Faries, Nathan. *The "Inscrutably Chinese" Church: How Narratives and Nationalism Continue to Divide Christianity*. Langham, MD: Lexington, 2010.

Gan, Hector. "Beijing Plans to Continue Tightening its Grip on Christianity and Islam as China Pushes Ahead with the 'Sinicization of Religion.'" *South China Morning Post*, March 6, 2019. https://www.scmp.com/news/china/politics/article/2188752/no-let-chinas-push-sinicise-religion-despite-global-outcry-over.

Hunter, Alan, and Kim-Kwong Chan. *Protestantism in Contemporary China*. Cambridge Studies in Ideology and Religion. Cambridge: Cambridge University Press, 1993.

Johnson, Ian. "How the State is Co-opting Religion in China." *Foreign Affairs*, January 7, 2019. https://www.foreignaffairs.com/articles/china/2019–01–07/how-state-co-opting-religion-china/.

Kindopp, Jason, and Carol Lee Hamrin, eds. *God and Caesar in China*. Washington, DC: Brookings Institution, 2004.

Koesel, Karrie J. *Religion and Authoritarianism: Cooperation, Conflict, and the Consequences*. Cambridge: Cambridge University Press, 2014.

Li, Ma. *Religious Entrepreneurism in China's Urban Churches: The Rise and Fall of Early Rain Reformed Presbyterian Church*. Routledge Studies in Religion. New York: Routledge 2019.

Li, Ma, and Jin Li. *Surviving the State, Remaking the Church*. Studies in Chinese Christianity. Eugene, OR: Pickwick Publications, 2018.

Lim, Francis Khek Gee, ed. *Christianity In Contemporary China*. Routledge Studies in Asian Religion and Philosophy 5. New York: Routledge, 2013.

Pittman, Joann. "Public Transcripts and Official Agendas." *ChinaSource*, April 30, 2018. https://www.chinasource.org/resource-library/blog-entries/public-transcripts-and-official-agendas/.

———. "Sinicization of Christianity—Understanding the Contexts." *ChinaSource* (blog). March 29, 2019.

Powers, John. "China's Religion Problem: Why the Chinese Communist Party Views Religious Belief as a Threat." *The Asia Dialogue*, October 17, 2019. https://theasiadialogue.com/2019/10/17/chinas-religion-problem-why-the-chinese-communist-party-views-religious-belief-as-a-threat/.

Qiao, Long, Siu-san Wong, and Kwok-lap Lam. "China Escalates Nationwide Crackdown on Protestant Churches." Edited and translated by Luisetta Mudie. *Radio Free Asia*, May 17, 2018. https://www.rfa.org/english/news/china/churches-05172018111646.html.

Schottelkorb, Kerry, and Joann Pittman. "China Tells Christianity to Be More Chinese." *Christianity Today*, March 20, 2019. https://www.christianitytoday.com/news/2019/march/sinicization-china-wants-christianity-churches-more-chinese.html/.

Selles, Kurt. "Through the Narrow Gate: Celebrating Christmas In China." *Reformed Worship* 73 (September 2004).

Spence, Jonathan. *God's Chinese Son: The Tai-Ping Heavenly Kingdom of Hong Xiuquan.* New York: Norton, 1997.

Stetzer, Ed. "Calling for Contextualization, Part 5: Indiginization." *The Exchange* (blog), August 2010. https://www.christianitytoday.com/edstetzer/2010/august/calling-for-contextualization-part-5-indigenization.html.

Swells in the Middle Kingdom. "Churches, Posters, and State Propaganda." *ChinaSource* (blog), November 25, 2019. https://www.chinasource.org/resource-library/blog-entries/churches-posters-and-state-propaganda/.

Ten Harmsel, Wayne. "The Challenge of Being the Church in China." *ChinaSource.* December 17, 2018. https://www.chinasource.org/resource-library/blog-entries/the-challenge-of-being-the-church-in-china/.

Towery, Britt. *Churches of China.* Waco, TX: Baylor University Press, 1990.

Vala, Carsten T. *The Politics of Protestant Churches and The Party-State in China: God Above Party?* New York: Routledge, 2018.

Werner, Burklin. *Jesus Never Left China.* Enumclaw, WA: Pleasant Word, 2005.

Wickeri, Philip. *Reconstructing Christianity in China: K. H. Ting and the Chinese Church.* American Society of Missiology Series 41. Maryknoll, NY: Orbis, 2007.

———. *Seeking the Common Ground.* Maryknoll, NY: Orbis, 1988.

Wielander, Gerda. *Christian Values in Communist China.* Routledge Contemporary China Series 109. New York: Routledge, 2013.

Wu, Jackson. "China's Five-Year Plan for Adapting Christianity to Chinese Socialism. *Pathos* (blog), May 23, 2018. https://www.patheos.com/blogs/jacksonwu/2018/05/23/chinas-five-year-plan-adapting-christianity-chinese-socialism/.

———. "Sinicized Christianity Is not Christianity." *Patheos* (blog), March 20, 2019. https://www.patheos.com/blogs/jacksonwu/2019/03/20/sinicized-christianity-is-not-christianity/.

———. "7 Reasons Why Sinicization Is not Rhetoric This Time." *ChinaSource* (blog). May 1, 2019. https://www.chinasource.org/resource-library/blog-entries/7-reasons-why-sinicization-is-not-rhetoric-this-time/.

Yang, C. K. *Religion in Chinese Society.* Prospect Heights, IL: Waveland, 1961.

Yang, Fenggang. *Religion in China: Survival and Revival under Communist Rule.* Oxford: Oxford University Press, 2012.

Yi, Yang "Sichuan Gospel Hospital Starts from Mustard Seed Faith, Now Serves Entire Community." *China Christian Daily.* June 1, 2018. http://chinachristiandaily.com/news/ministry/2018-06-01/sichuan-gospel-hospital-starts-from-mustered-seed-faith-now-serves-entire-community_7250/.

www.ingramcontent.com/pod-product-compliance
Lightning Source LLC
Chambersburg PA
CBHW060344100426
42812CB00003B/1125